You watch a lot of televi... ...some might even call you a couch potato ... In fact you think you're pretty clued up when it comes to matters of the telly ... Okay – now is your chance to prove it!

Which show featured La Di Da Gunner Graham?

Which classical actress said that appearing on *The Morecambe and Wise Show* was the highlight of her career?

Who told us to 'watch out there's a Humphrey about'?

When preparing a Christmas meal, what did Mr Bean get his head stuck inside?

How did *Coronation Street*'s Derek cause a flood in the Kabin?

ABOUT THE AUTHORS

Former newspaper journalists Chris Pointer and Alison Fitzpatrick have been members of the features staff of *TVTimes* for six years and devise the weekly crossword and TV quiz for the magazine. They have compiled the questions and puzzles for this book after extensive research from a wide variety of sources – not to mention a great deal of time spent watching television. Both Chris and Alison are married with children and would like to thank their husbands Richard and Matt plus Anna, Kate, Nicky, Jamie and Theo for all their help, patience and inspiration.

Chris and Alison have also compiled *Your Favourite Soaps Puzzle and Quiz Book*.

The Signet Television Puzzle and Quiz Book

Chris Pointer
and
Alison Fitzpatrick

A SIGNET BOOK

SIGNET

Published by the Penguin Group
Penguin Books Ltd, 27 Wrights Lane, London W8 5TZ, England
Penguin Books USA Inc., 375 Hudson Street, New York, New York 10014, USA
Penguin Books Australia Ltd, Ringwood, Victoria, Australia
Penguin Books Canada Ltd, 10 Alcorn Avenue, Toronto, Ontario, Canada M4V 3B2
Penguin Books (NZ) Ltd, 182–190 Wairau Road, Auckland 10, New Zealand

Penguin Books Ltd, Registered Offices: Harmondsworth, Middlesex, England

First published 1994
1 3 5 7 9 10 8 6 4 2

The moral right of the authors has been asserted

All pictures courtesy of *TVTimes* picture library

Typeset by Datix International Limited, Bungay, Suffolk
Filmset in 10/13pt Monophoto Plantin
Printed in England by Clays Ltd, St Ives plc

Contents

COMEDY

Television has provided lots of laughs over the years. So how much do you remember about comedy shows both past and present and the comedians who made us smile?

Vintage Comedy

A1   What role did Richard Beckinsale play in *Porridge*?

A2   What was Fletcher's middle name?

A3   What was the name of the follow-up series that had Fletch coming out of jail?

A4   Where did the old boys fight the war from in *Dad's Army*?

A5   What was Captain Mainwaring's day-time job?

A6   What was local butcher Jones' Home Guard rank?

A7   What was Captain Mainwaring's favourite description for Private Pike?

A8   In *Till Death Us Do Part* what did Alf Garnett call his wife?

A9   What was his daughter's name and who played her?

A10 Who were Tom and Barbara's snooty neighbours in *The Good Life*?

A11 What did Barbara name their two pigs?

A12 What was the name of Basil's terrifying wife in *Fawlty Towers*?

A13 Where did waiter Manuel come from?

A14 What did Basil unsuccessfully try to avoid mentioning in front of his German guests?

A15 What did Basil do to his car when it broke down at a vital moment during the hotel's Gourmet Night?

B1 What was the name of Penelope Keith's upper-crust character in *To the Manor Born*?

B2 Who was her butler?

B3 What was the name of the manor house in the show?

B4 What was the nationality of the new lord of the manor's mother?

B5 What was the name of the store in *Are You Being Served*?

B6 What is the connection between the show and *EastEnders*?

B7 Who played the camp Mr Humphries?

B8 Which department did Mrs Slocombe work in?

B9 Which big screen star was one of the original *Liver Birds*?

B10 What was the name of Nerys Hughes' character and who was her blonde flatmate?

B11 What were Wendy Craig's two sons called in *Butterflies*?

B12 Geoffrey Palmer played her long-suffering husband. What was his profession and in which other comedy did he play a loony major?

B13 What was Wendy Craig's name in *Butterflies* and what was the distinguishing feature of her Mini?

B14 Name the 'childish' show that Wendy Craig created and starred in.

B15 What comedy show saw Hannah Gordon as a bank manager and Peter Egan as her husband?

C1 In *Fresh Fields* who was the nosey next-door neighbour?

C2 Which country did the Fields move to in the follow-up series?

C3 Name the sitcom featuring Sid Abbott, a stationery sales rep baffled by the generation gap between himself and his workshy son and teenage schoolgirl daughter. Who was the popular comedy actor who played Sid?

C4 What was the name of the busybody played by Richard Briers in *Ever Decreasing Circles*?

C5 Every episode of *It Ain't Half Hot, Mum* ended with a wailing version of which British song?

C6 What were the nicknames of brainy Gunner Graham and Bombardier Beaumont?

C7 In *Rising Damp* who was the lodger Rigsby lusted after?

C8 What was Richard Beckinsale's student Alan studying?

C9 What was the name of Rigsby's cat?

C10 What was the trade of Steptoe and Son?

C11 What was their horse called?

C12 Who were the two actors who played the lead roles?

C13 Name the MP Paul Eddington played in *Yes, Minister* and who was his Permanent Under-Secretary played by Nigel Hawthorne?

C14 Who was Stan's sister in *On the Buses*?

C15 What was the name of his conductor pal?

Comedians

D1   In which show did Morecambe and Wise make their début?

D2   What were the comedy duo's real names?

D3   Which classical actress said that appearing on *The Morecambe and Wise Show* was the highlight of her career?

D4   Which newsreader caused a sensation when she did a high-kicking dance routine with Eric and Ernie?

D5   What name do Hale and Pace's two tough-nut characters go by?

D6   Dawn French and Jennifer Saunders both have famous husbands. Who are they?

D7   Both French and Saunders went on to star independently in comedies – name the shows.

D8   What was the late Seventies alternative comedy show Mel Smith and Griff Rhys Jones first appeared together in?

D9   What tasty series saw Mel Smith playing a British Rail complaints clerk?

D10   What costume drama series did Stephen Fry and Hugh Laurie appear together in?

D11   What was the catchphrase of Dick Emery's buxom creation Mandy?

D12   Who among the royal family is said to be the biggest fan of *The Two Ronnies*?

D13   What was the name of the sitcom that Ronnie Corbett went on to star in as wimpy mummy's boy Timothy?

D14   At which address was *Hancock's Half Hour* set?

D15   Who was Tony Hancock's sparring partner?

General Comedy

E1   Name the writer of *Only Fools and Horses*.
E2   What is Del's address?
E3   What is the name of Del's favourite pub and who is the landlord?
E4   What colour is Del's van and what words appear along the side?
E5   What is Rodney's wife called?
E6   What is Del's favourite saying?
E7   In *Keeping Up Appearances* what is the name of Hyacinth's slobby brother-in-law?
E8   Where did Hyacinth's husband Richard work?
E9   Who are Hyacinth's neighbours?
E10   What does Hyacinth say when she answers the telephone?
E11   Name Hyacinth's sisters.
E12   What did Hyacinth call her son and who did she name him after?
E13   Name the woman Hyacinth looks up to and who also helps out at the charity shop.
E14   What social occasion is Hyacinth's particular pride and joy?
E15   What subject did Hyacinth's son take up in place of maths?

F1   What was Ma Boswell's first name in *Bread*?
F2   Who was Aveline's husband and what was his profession?
F3   Who was Freddie Boswell's passion and where did they meet for romance?

F4 What is the name of the leisure centre in *The Brittas Empire*?

F5 Who is the receptionist who keeps her children under the counter?

F6 Where did Helen Brittas give birth to her twins?

F7 What are Malcolm and Brenda's surnames in *Watching*?

F8 What role did Patsy Byrne (Malcolm's mum) play in *Blackadder*?

F9 Who did Malcolm marry instead of Brenda?

F10 What is the name of Brenda's snobby sister?

F11 Name the café owner and his wife in *'Allo 'Allo*.

F12 Who does the mean Herr Flick have a passion for?

F13 What was the painting featured in many episodes that the Resistance fighters were desperately trying to hide?

F14 What is the name of the secret serviceman posing as a gendarme and what is his favourite greeting?

F15 Who is the leader of the Resistance and what is her favourite saying?

G1 Which US show was *Brighton Belles* based on?

G2 What is the connection between a dark viper and a vegetable?

G3 Who was the 'boy' that Blackadder II fell for?

G4 Who was Blackadder's stupid servant?

G5 Who played the outrageous Lord Flashheart in *Blackadder II*?

G6 What was Stephen Fry's role in the final *Blackadder* series?

G7 Name Fry's sidekick with a lovely name.

G8 How did the last episode end?

G9 What was the name of the holiday camp in *Hi-De-Hi*?

G10 Who was the chambermaid who dreamed of becoming a yellowcoat?

G11 Who took over as entertainments manager when Jeffrey Fairbrother left?

G12 Who were the snooty ballroom dancers?

G13 In *Birds of a Feather* what is the name of Tracey's son?

G14 What were Darryl and Chris jailed for?

G15 Which US movie star did Sharon and Tracey once think was their father?

H1 What is Victor Meldrew's favourite saying in *One Foot in the Grave*?

H2 Before he retired, what job did Victor have for twenty-six years?

H3 What is Mrs Meldrew's first name?

H4 Which news man plays the Meldrews' neighbour?

H5 What is the name of Mrs Meldrew's gossipy friend?

H6 Why did Victor once have to wear a blindfold in bed?

H7 Who did Victor rescue after a day in the country when he became marooned on a lake?

H8 How did Mrs Meldrew cover Victor's embarrassment when he was buried up to his neck in the garden?

H9 In *Waiting for God*, what is the name of the retirement home and who runs it?

H10 What are the surnames of Tom and Diana?

H11 Name the sex-mad pensioner.

H12 Who is the matron and how did her boss break her heart after he attended the hunt ball?

H13 What sort of car does Mr Bean drive?

H14 When preparing a Christmas meal, what did Mr Bean get his head stuck inside?

H15 When Mr Bean went to the beach how did he prepare to go swimming?

I1 What is Edina's job in *Absolutely Fabulous*?

I2 What is Patsy's job?

I3 Who is Edina's favourite fashion designer?

I4 What happened when Edina and Patsy went on holiday to France?

I5 When they returned from France, Patsy was stopped in Customs for possessing an illegal substance. What did it turn out to be?

I6 What is the name of Edina's secretary?

I7 What trendy aid to relaxation did Edina have installed in her bathroom?

I8 Who played Shelley?

I9 Name Shelley's wife and daughter.

I10 What academic qualification does Shelley hold?

I11 Which one-time Minder went *On the Up*?

I12 What is the name of the housekeeper in *On the Up* and what is her catchphrase?

I13 What business does Tony Carpenter run?

I14 Name the show in which comedian Jim Davidson played a chauffeur.

I15 What sort of shop does Desmond run in the comedy of the same name?

J1 Who are Faith's two children in *Second Thoughts*?

J2 Name the older man who became so besotted by Liza that he left his wife.

J3 What is the name of Faith's dog?

J4   What is Ben's occupation in *2point4 children*?

J5   Who is Bill's least favourite politician?

J6   Why did the family think they were in deadly danger when they went on holiday to Florida?

J7   Why didn't they attend Rona's wedding?

J8   In *The Upper Hand* what was Charlie's former profession and why did he give it up?

J9   Where were Caroline and Charlie when they realized it must be love?

J10 In which Yorkshire village is *Last of the Summer Wine* filmed?

J11 Who is the woman of Compo's dreams and what is she famed for?

J12 What was Compo's ambition that involved his beloved's bedroom?

J13 When Foggy inherited his uncle's painted egg business where did he move to?

J14 Which famous soap star became a member of the *Last of the Summer Wine* cast?

J15 What was Clegg's former job?

US Comedy

If you're a fan of American humour, try these questions on US shows.

K1   In *Roseanne* what is the name of the eldest daughter?

K2   What is Roseanne and Dan's surname?

K3   Where do the family live?

K4   In which US city was *Cheers* set?

K5   What was the name of the beer-supping postman who still lives with his mother?

K6   To which big screen star is *Cheers* barmaid Carla married in real life?

K7   Which dippy Golden Girl came from St Olaf?

K8   Which Golden Girl quit when her pals left to set up the Golden Palace?

K9   What was the name of the family the Fonz had a soft spot for in *Happy Days*?

K10 Who is Cliff Huxtable's son in *The Cosby Show*?

K11 Which programme did Rhoda first appear in?

K12 What was her job and where did she live?

K13 What was the name of the doorman whose voice was heard on the entryphone?

K14 What was Lucy's surname before she married Ricky in *I Love Lucy*?

K15 What did Ricky do for a living?

Comedy Crossword

It might be a challenge – but keep on smiling as you tackle our comedy crossword.

Across

1 Hawkeye, Hotlips, Radar and Trapper John – you'll find them all in this US war comedy (1,1,1,1)

3 As Norman Stanley Fletcher, Ronnie Barker served plenty of this (8)

9 Derek — , he's *All Gas and Gaiters* (5)

10 *Carry On* hero Mr James (3)

11 The role Paul Nicholas played with an animal passion (3)

12 You'll find he's always Bean behind Blackadder (5)

14 The wide-boy star of *Only Fools and Horses* (3)

15 Stanley – the Scottish comedian who had a Big Picture Show back in the Seventies (6)

17 *Q* Mr Milligan – or even one of the *Hi-De-Hi* yellowcoats (5)

20 First name of a sweet-smelling *Dad's Army* star (3)

22 Chris Evans and Julia McKenzie can both be described as this, up top (3,4)

25 James Bolam's Likely Lad – in full! (7)

26 The number of feet Victor Meldrew had in the grave (3)

27 Arthur Daley likes a nice little one! (6)

28 Mr Morecambe's clever pal (4)

Down

1 It's what Penelope Keith was born to (5)

2 *Cheers!* It's the girl-mad bar owner (3)

4 The slob of a brother-in-law who certainly doesn't help Hyacinth keep up appearances (6)

5 The last name of the man who went from *Fresh Fields* to *May to December* (7)

6 The man who's married to Brenda's sister in *Watching* (5)

7 *It Ain't Half Hot, Mum* for little Don (7)

8 Harry Secombe and Michael Bentine are both an ex one (4)

13 Motormouth funnygirl Ruby (3)

15 The bungling manager of that famous leisure centre empire (7)

16 Joan Sanderson's overbearing mum in *After Henry* (7)

18 For the love of Ada, it's — Handl (5)

19 *Rising Damp* may have caused miserly landlord Rigsby a problem but he'd be sure to do this when the weather turned cold (6)

21 It's the profession of Arkwright's intended in *Open All Hours* (5)

23 What you'd do to the dead donkey (4)

24 The pint-sized funnyman who's a proper Charlie (5)

Comedy Wordsearch

Put your TV comedy knowledge to the test. Take a look at the following questions and see if you can find the answers in the wordsearch.

As with all the wordsearch puzzles in this book, you will find some of the words are hidden back to front and diagonally too.

1 What was Felicity Kendal's role in *The Good Life*? (7)
2 Who was the man behind Mr Humphries in *Are You Being Served*? (4,5)
3 Which famous comedy writer penned *The Liver Birds*, *Butterflies* and *Bread*? (5,4)
4 Name the oldest of Roseanne's three children. (5)
5 Who plays the interfering mother in *The Upper Hand*? (5,8)
6 What was the name of Basil Fawlty's wife? (5)
7 What was the prison called in *Porridge*? (5)
8 Where do the *Birds of a Feather* live? (8)
9 What is Malcolm's hobby in *Watching*? (12)
10 Name the manor house in *Mulberry* (7)
11 Which *Have I Got News for You* star has his own comedy series? (4,6)
12 Who is the woman of Compo's dreams? (4,5)
13 Kevin Arnold is the central character in which US show? (3,6,5)
14 Name Rik Mayall's rampantly right-wing MP (4,6)
15 Who are French and Saunders' resident musicians? (3,3)

14

B	P	A	U	L	M	E	R	T	O	N	T
M	A	E	D	A	L	S	R	H	A	O	T
E	I	R	A	I	P	C	L	O	N	T	H
J	T	G	B	C	E	A	L	N	O	O	E
O	P	Y	D	A	B	R	O	O	R	D	W
H	S	B	T	M	R	L	O	R	A	R	O
N	C	A	D	O	E	A	R	B	B	A	N
I	U	N	R	N	O	L	L	L	A	T	D
N	F	R	J	M	P	A	T	A	T	S	E
M	A	A	H	C	P	N	L	C	T	B	R
A	N	F	Y	K	C	E	B	K	Y	N	Y
N	T	O	R	L	T	O	R	M	E	A	E
T	C	H	I	X	E	S	W	A	R	L	A
C	H	I	G	W	E	L	L	N	O	A	R
R	A	O	N	S	A	X	E	V	S	P	S
B	I	R	D	W	A	T	C	H	I	N	G

Comedy Star Anagrams

Hidden in the anagrams below are some of our top comedy stars. See if you can unravel them – the clues should give you a hand.

1 HIDE BR CAR, SIRR: He's had a good life going round in circles.

2 I EAT CARROT LEG UP, DI: A flowery snob, it appears.

3 DON'T GLUE PAD IN: One of the minister's men? Yes, sir!

4 IN RANK OR BEER: He never shuts up shop.

5 R U LOW HEART?: Who do you think you are kidding, Captain?

6 SH, CLEEN JOE: Things weren't working at his hotel.

7 HIM SMELT: Alas, he's got to keep up with Jones.

8 BEAT JOHN: She enjoyed a slice of Brighton life.

9 WHY LE NET BENT?: He's no poet, just a lovable layabout.

10 YES, ER SICK: A funnyman you might find at the nineteenth hole.

11 ROY SHUNN LAST CHILD: The plonker who grew up with the two of us.

12 A CALM WORD CHIEF R: Whoopsie, it's Betty's boy.

13 OBE SLAM JAM: A lad who had second thoughts.

14 NEAR MR WET CHILL: Whether he's sick or in good health, he's still a pain.

15 THE REGAL HA: A man who keeps Pace with his partner.

COLOURFUL CHARACTERS

The following characters are sure to ring a bell. But can you remember which shows they came from?

1 Richard De Vere
2 Sir Humphrey Appleby
3 Siegfried Farnon
4 Guy Pringle
5 Arnie Becker
6 Martin Ashford
7 Dave Quinnan
8 Colin Weatherby
9 Tony Wilton
10 Laura West
11 Sam Malone
12 Diana Trent
13 Billy Boswell
14 Robbie Box
15 George Smiley

THE DETECTIVES

Are you clued up on detective shows both past and present? Then investigate this section and see how many questions you can crack.

A1 What were the two towns featured in *Z Cars* and which real city were they supposed to be near?

A2 Who played PC David Graham and which film did he later win an Oscar for writing?

A3 What is the connection between *Z Cars* and the children's show *Rainbow*?

A4 Which two officers left *Z Cars* to tread *Softly, Softly* in 1966?

A5 Why was *Z Cars* cop PC Smith known as Fancy?

A6 How did *The Sweeney* get its name?

A7 Name Jack Regan's boss in *The Sweeney*.

A8 Stephanie Turner, who played Dennis Waterman's wife, went on to star in another top police series. Name the series and also name Waterman's *Sweeney* role.

A9 Which comedy duo starred as themselves in the final series of *The Sweeney*?

A10 What was Jack Regan's favourite phrase when nabbing the bad guys?

A11 What was the name of *The Professionals*' crime-busting unit?

A12 What were Bodie and Doyle's jobs before they became Professionals?

A13 Who was their tough boss and who played him?

A14 What were Bodie and Doyle nicknamed by their chief?

A15 What more sedate crime-busting role did Martin Shaw eventually take up?

B1 On which radio station did Shoestring host a phone-in show?

B2 Who played the radio station's secretary and who is her famous dad?

B3 Why was doubt sometimes expressed over Shoestring's health?

B4 *Shoestring* actor Trevor Eve went on to play a womanizing writer in which BBC series? And what was the name of his character?

B5 In which town and county was *Juliet Bravo* set and who were the two characters who have headed the Juliet Bravo force?

B6 What was the name of the police station where Detective Inspector Maggie Forbes worked in *The Gentle Touch* and which area of London was it supposed to be close to?

B7 Who was the actress who played Maggie and in which other crime-fighting series did she take the lead role?

B8 In which film did the *Dixon of Dock Green* character first appear?

B9 What was the name of Dixon's daughter and who was his son-in-law?

B10 What was George Dixon's famous greeting?

B11 In *Dempsey and Makepeace*, where did Dempsey come from?

B12 Which university had Makepeace been to and what did she study?

B13 Name the two leading actors.

B14 Who played the tough taskmaster in *Rockcliffe's Babies*?

B15 What was the name of the follow-up series?

C1 What is Inspector Morse's favourite tipple?

C2 What was the job of Morse's female colleague, Grayling Russell, who he became rather attached to?

C3 Who is Morse's boss, played by James Grout?

C4 Why did Morse never marry?

C5 What does Morse hate to see?

C6 When following up a case in Italy what was the profession of the woman Morse was smitten with?

C7 Name the village and the northern county in which *Heartbeat* is set.

C8 Name the local poacher.

C9 Who is the bad-tempered sergeant and what is his connection to a small fox and 10 Downing Street?

C10 What is the name of Poirot's secretary?

C11 What part of himself does Poirot describe as the finest in London?

C12 What is Poirot's London address?

C13 Who played Maigret in the Nineties and what other sort of detective has he played?

C14 Who created Maigret and where was he born?

C15 Who played Maigret in the Sixties TV series?

D1 Which top detective is also a poet?

D2 Which famous mystery writer created him?

D3 Who played Spender and in which TV series did he make his name?

D4 Who is Spender's law-breaking sidekick?

D5 What happened to Spender's wife at the end of the last series?

D6 Where is Detective Chief Inspector Reg Wexford's home patch?

D7 Name Wexford's assistant.

D8 In which city did Taggart fight crime?

D9 What are the names of Taggart's wife and daughter?

D10 Name Taggart's assistant.

D11 In one of his most famous cases Taggart was on the trail of a murderous butcher. What did the butcher do with the bodies?

D12 What is the name of the Jersey police unit that Bergerac worked for?

D13 Who was his father-in-law and which actor played him?

D14 Who was the woman diamond thief played by Liza Goddard who popped up on several occasions?

D15 What happened to Bergerac when he resigned from the Jersey Force?

E1 What is the name of the police station in *The Bill*?

E2 A set once had to be built inside a cage for a story featuring DC Mike Dashwood. Why?

E3 Who is known as the station's resident whinger?

E4 Name *The Bill*'s Chief Superintendent.

E5 When was the first episode of *The Bill* broadcast?

E6 What major change happened to the series in January 1993?

E7 What is the station's radio signal sign that's used with numbers for panda cars and personnel?

E8 What happened to Viv Martella?

E9 Why did detective Tony Scannell exit in disgrace?

E10 How did PC Ken Melvin die?

E11 When Hollis thought he'd discovered a multiple murder after coming across a load of bones in a flat, what was the innocent explanation?

E12 Which actor played Van der Valk and where was this policeman's beat?

E13 What was the *Van der Valk* theme tune that was top of the charts in 1973 and who recorded it?

E14 Who was the arch enemy of Sherlock Holmes?

E15 Until his unexpected return, where was Holmes thought to have died?

F1 In *Between the Lines* what was the name of Tony Clark's department?

F2 Name Clark's two assistants.

F3 Who was the woman from the Home Office with whom Clark became involved in the second series and who played her?

F4 What was the main difference in the portrayal of Tony Clark between the first and second series?

F5 Which comedy actor played a cracking crime-buster?

F6 What is his job?

F7 Name the Chief Inspector who Fitz works for.

F8 What is Fitz's nickname for Detective Sergeant Penhaligon?

F9 What are Fitz's three main vices?

F10 In which series did Detective Inspector Ronald Craven seek to find the killers of his daughter Emma?

F11 Who were the two Saintly actors?

F12 Which detective series starred David Yip battling the villains in Liverpool?

F13 Which show first featured Don Henderson as Bulman?

F14 Which Sixties series centred on Chief Superintendent Lockhart?

F15 What do television cops Nick Berry, David Soul and Telly Savalas have in common?

G1 What were the Christian names of crime-fighting Cagney and Lacey?

G2 In *Hill Street Blues* who was the lawyer Captain Furillo ended up in bed with at the end of every episode?

G3 Which city did Seventies favourites Starsky and Hutch patrol?

G4 What was the name of their trendy club-owning pal?

G5 Which US singing superstar was first choice as Columbo?

G6 Who did the role go to?

G7 What sweets was Kojak addicted to?

G8 What was his New York City beat?

G9 What was the real connection between Kojak and his detective Stavros?

G10 Who were the two undercover cops in *Miami Vice*?

G11 What was the former job of Don Johnson's character?

G12 What unusual pet did he keep?

G13 Who was the glamorous cop in *Police Woman* and who played her?

G14 Which Charlie's Angel married a Six Million Dollar Man?

G15 What was the name of Jim Rockford's dad in *The Rockford Files* and who was his policeman pal?

The Crime-busters Crossword

Across

1 First name of detective who worked with 2 Down (4)

3 Holiday island policeman (8)

8 Clever chap who knows the code on ale and opera (5)

9 The detective from Kingsmarkham (7)

10 North East detective who sounds as if he likes to go shopping (7)

12 Police action in short that could be carried out in the theatre (2)

16 He may be brilliant in court, but who must Rumpole obey? (3)

18 Villains don't stand a chance against the glamorous — Lee, played by Imogen Stubbs (4)

21 When Fitz is backing the horses of course he needs a muddled ray of inspiration (3)

22 If it's murder, you can't fool this man in the big mac (7)

24 Patrick Malahide plays this upper-class detective with an arty friend (6)

25 Last letter in transport for the TV cops in this long-running series (4)

27 Helen Mirren had a prime role as this tough lady cop (8)

28 Policeman's rhythm – specially Nick Rowan's (4)

Down

1 Mr Macpherson who played right-hand man to 15 Down (5)

2 Dennis Waterman's *Sweeney* role (6)

4 First name of actor whose bank balance received a big plus when he became the Equalizer (6)

5 Hardly party fun when the crowd goes wild and police are called in (4)

6 No uniforms in this branch, initially (1,1,1)

7 Find a body like this and it could be murder (4)

11 Commonly a trick that perhaps Detective Sergeant Chisholm would love to have pinned on Arthur Daley (3)

13 He solves crimes with the help of his little grey cells (6)

14 Musician Jan who hit the charts with 'Crockett's Theme' from US cop show *Miami Vice* (6)

15 Gritty Glasgow detective (7)

17 O, so this was the crime-buster played by David Janssen (5)

19 Downbeat Sixties crimefighter played by 4 Down (6)

20 Chilly, a bit like David Jason's Detective Inspector Jack Frost perhaps (3)

23 A criminal is put under this with a key (4)

26 Angelic Roger Moore fought the baddies in abbreviated form (2)

Detectives Wordsearch

How good are you at solving a mystery? The following crime-busters are hiding out in the wordsearch – but one has gone missing. See if you can work out which one it is.

Taggart	Wexford
Spender	Sherlock Holmes
Shoestring	Maigret
Poirot	Jessica Fletcher
Miss Marple	Columbo
Cagney and Lacey	Cannon
Starsky and Hutch	Ironside
Bergerac	Kojak
Morse	Magnum
T.J. Hooker	The Professionals

M	E	A	P	T	R	A	G	G	A	T	O
Y	M	L	C	K	O	J	A	K	J	H	H
E	A	S	P	S	R	E	D	B	H	E	C
C	G	E	P	H	R	S	L	E	O	P	T
A	N	M	O	O	S	S	M	R	C	R	U
L	U	L	I	E	W	I	O	G	J	O	H
D	M	O	R	S	E	C	R	E	E	F	D
N	D	H	O	T	X	A	T	R	D	E	N
A	R	K	T	R	F	F	O	A	I	S	A
Y	E	C	E	I	O	L	B	C	S	S	Y
E	D	O	R	N	R	E	M	A	N	I	K
N	N	L	G	G	D	T	U	N	O	O	S
G	E	R	I	O	J	C	L	N	R	N	R
A	P	E	A	O	R	H	O	O	I	A	A
C	S	H	M	K	T	E	C	N	I	L	T
M	I	S	S	M	A	R	P	L	E	S	S

COMMERCIAL BREAK

It's time for a commercial break. See how much you can remember about TV ads both past and present.

A1 Which was the very first commercial broadcast on ITV?

A2 Which television bear gave his backing to OXO in the Fifties?

A3 Who is the 'bootiful' Norfolk turkey farmer?

A4 Which drink did Lorraine Chase down at Luton Airport?

A5 In a phone ad, John Cleese and Ronnie Corbett put on wigs and frocks to impersonate which top comedy actress?

A6 Who is Papa's girl in the Renault Clio ads?

A7 Which soft drink declared 'I'd Like to Teach the World to Sing'?

A8 Which beer worked wonders according to the advertisers?

A9 Which was the petrol for getaway people in 1964?

A10 How much stronger were Trebor mints?

A11 The Milk Tray man got a softer image in the 1993 Christmas TV ad campaign. He gave her the usual chocolates but what did his lady love give him?

A12 What did a million housewives every day pick up and say?

A13 Who told us to 'watch out, there's a Humphrey about'?

A14 Which drink did Leonard Rossiter pour over Joan Collins?

A15 Who was the first British athlete to allow his name to be used to promote products on television – and what was the product?

CATCHPHRASES

'Nice to see you, to see you nice' – everyone knows Brucie's favourite saying. But can you remember who's responsible for the following catchphrases?

1 'We're doomed, we're doomed.'
2 'I 'ate you, Butler.'
3 'Evenin' all.'
4 'Who loves ya, baby?'
5 'Book 'em, Danno.'
6 'How's about that, then.'
7 'Phenomenal.'
8 'I don't believe it.'
9 'It's goodnight from me and it's goodnight from him.'
10 'And here's one I made earlier.'
11 'What do you think of it so far?'
12 'May your God go with you.'
13 'I like it, not a lot.'
14 'You wouldn't let it lie.'
15 'How tickled I am.'

DRAMA

British television is famed all around the world for its high-quality drama. Put your memory to the test with these questions that include the classics such as *The Jewel in the Crown* and more recent shows like *Casualty* and *Minder*.

A1 What is the name of the fire station in *London's Burning*?

A2 How did Sicknote and Vaseline get their nicknames?

A3 Which watch do the boys belong to?

A4 Vaseline was married three times. His first and third wife both had the same name. What was it?

A5 How did Vaseline die?

A6 Who once took over from Bayleaf in the mess and why did his menu result in outrage among the men?

A7 Which writer came up with the idea for *London's Burning* and who is his famous wife?

A8 What did George take up to try to meet the girl of his dreams?

A9 What happened to Bayleaf and Hallam when they attended a massive warehouse blaze?

A10 Name the fire-fighter who moonlights as a plumber and a male stripper.

A11 What was the big shock that Kelly sprang on George in their honeymoon suite?

A12 How did Colin and Zoe meet?

A13 When Colin and Zoe got married, what did the men use to form a guard of honour arch for them to walk through?

A14 What was Geoffrey Pearce's nickname and why?

A15 Ladies man Billy Ray had an unusual passion wagon. What was it?

B1 What is the name of the hospital in *Casualty*?

B2 Which doctor and nurse had a fling in the autumn 1992 series?

B3 What was Charlie's title in the casualty unit?

B4 Who played a motherly Irish nurse in the first series of *Casualty*? She won an Oscar for her performance in which film?

B5 What was the name of the popular surgeon who died suddenly of a heart attack?

B6 Which MP branded the show left-wing propaganda when it first started – and why?

B7 What happened in the episode that caused national outrage and claims that the series was too violent?

B8 What was Duffy desperate to achieve in autumn 1993?

B9 Who was the porter who quit the show to join the army?

B10 What was the original name of the regiment the boys in *Soldier, Soldier* belonged to?

B11 What was the new name of the regiment and why did it change?

B12 After the two regiments merged what was the bitter uniform fight over?

B13 Why did Nancy and Paddy's marriage fall apart?

B14 What is the name of Dave and Donna's son?

B15 What lasting memory of a night out in Amsterdam was Sergeant Tony Wilton left with?

C1 Which year first saw *Minder* on our screens?

C2 What is the name of Arthur Daley's favourite drinking club?

C3 What is Arthur's favourite drink?

C4 What is Arthur's name for the police?

C5 Who was the detective always on Arthur's trail when the show first started?

C6 Who was Arthur's first Minder and what was his former profession?

C7 What phrase does Arthur use to describe a money-making venture?

C8 Who became Minder number two and what relation was he to Arthur?

C9 Why did Arthur go to Australia?

C10 Who was the upper-crust love of Lovejoy's life?

C11 Where were she and Lovejoy seen to be enjoying a romantic Highland fling?

C12 Who was the glamorous widow who had a romance with Lovejoy and which well-known actress played her?

C13 After the departure of Lady Jane, who did Lovejoy fall for and what was her job?

C14 Name Lovejoy's two assistants.

C15 *Lovejoy* actor Ian McShane shares the same taste in clothes as his screen character – what are the three things he always wears on and off-screen?

D1 In which decade is *The House of Eliott* set?

D2 Name the two sisters who founded the fashion house.

D3   Why did the sisters first set up in business?

D4   Where did Bea and Jack Maddox get married?

D5   What business did Jack become involved in?

D6   Why did Evie's affair with Alexander Montford cause a stir?

D7   What other series did Jean Marsh, who helped devise *The House of Eliott*, co-create and what was her role in it?

D8   In *Boon* what was Ken's job before he was invalided out to set up as a freelance trouble-shooter?

D9   What was the name of his motorbike despatch business?

D10 Who is his former colleague and best mate?

D11 Who was the leather-clad biker who helped him out in his investigations?

D12 *Boon* actor Michael Elphick went on to play another gritty character called Harry Salter. What was his job?

D13 What was the name of the stableyard in *Trainer*?

D14 Who sang the theme tune to *Trainer*?

D15 The BBC spent £30,000 on buying what for the *Trainer* series?

E1   Which show did Kevin Whately leave *Morse* for?

E2   Name his character and professional role.

E3   Which star of *Auf Wiedersehen, Pet* got his own comedy drama series in 1993?

E4   Name the characters he played in both shows.

E5   Which one-time pop star found out that *Love Hurts*?

E6   Who was his co-star and what role did she play?

E7   Which county is home to *The Darling Buds of May*?

E8 Who is the youngest of Ma and Pop Larkin's children?

E9 Before he married Mariette, what was Charley's job?

E10 What is Pop Larkin's favourite word to describe something good?

E11 Name the couple who fostered a whole host of children in *Growing Pains*.

E12 One of their charges – Jason – later became a familiar face in one of the top soaps. Name him, the soap and the role he played.

E13 Who played Dennis Waterman's first love in *Stay Lucky*?

E14 Which D.H. Lawrence novel was brought to life by Sean Bean and Joely Richardson?

E15 Which Scottish drama featured Alec and Jennifer Ritchie?

Vintage Drama

F1 Who played the lead role in *Jesus of Nazareth* and which comedian did he go on to team up with?

F2 What was the name and profession of Jeremy Irons' character in *Brideshead Revisited*?

F3 Name the real-life castle featured in the series.

F4 Who was Sebastian's father and which great actor played him?

F5 What was the name of Sebastian's teddy bear?

F6 In *The Jewel in the Crown* who was Daphne Manners' lover and who played him?

F7 Name the sadistic policeman Tim Pigott-Smith won a best-actor BAFTA for.

F8   Who was the homely cook in *Upstairs, Downstairs*?

F9   Which member of the cast turned Professional?

F10 Name the family the series featured.

F11 Two of the *Upstairs, Downstairs* cast married and went on to star in an environmentally friendly series of their own. Who were they and what was the show?

F12 Which drama was hailed the first royal soap – and who approved the scripts?

F13 Who played the lead role and who is his famous wife?

F14 Which former Australian art teacher won rave reviews for the lead role in *The Six Wives of Henry VIII*?

F15 Name the actresses who played the six wives.

G1   What nationality was James Aubrey in *A Bouquet of Barbed Wire*?

G2   What was the follow-up saga called?

G3   In *The Onedin Line* who was Captain James' faithful crewman?

G4   What was the name of the schooner in the series?

G5   Which was the last major series to be made in black and white?

G6   In *The Avengers*, Honor Blackman's appearance caused a sensation. Why?

G7   Honor Blackman and Diana Rigg, who played Emma Peel in *The Avengers*, both went on to have a common link in their film careers. What is it?

G8   Doctor Finlay has made a comeback – but who took the role in the original series?

G9   What is the name of the village where Doctor Finlay practises?

G10 Name the house where he lived with Doctor Cameron.

G11 What was the name of the hero in *The Saint* and which two actors played him?

G12 In *Howards' Way* what was the name of the boatyard run by Jack Rolfe?

G13 Who was the Howards' arch-enemy – and the man Jan Howard had a fling with?

G14 Name the rock 'n' roll drama starring Robbie Coltrane and Emma Thompson.

G15 In *All Creatures Great and Small* what was the name of the pampered Pekinese?

US Drama

H1 Who were the two brothers in *Rich Man, Poor Man* and who played them?

H2 What was the name of the family in *Little House on the Prairie*?

H3 Michael Landon played the father – which western series had he previously starred in?

H4 Which sixteen-hour £25-million series starred Robert Mitchum as US Navy officer Commander Pug Henry?

H5 What was the name of the African chief's son captured and taken to Virginia in *Roots*?

H6 Who was his grandson and what activity was he involved in?

H7 Who was the wayward Catholic priest in *The Thorn Birds* and who played him?

H8 Which war was the subject of the drama *North and South*?

H9 Who was the Waltons' oldest boy and what career did he pursue?

H10 Who starred as *The Fugitive* and which character did he play?

H11 Which US mini-series featured Lili, a porn star seeking revenge on an unknown mother for abandoning her?

H12 Which year saw the start of *Peyton Place*?

H13 Name the two stars of the show who went on to become big movie stars.

H14 Who was the bookstore owner in love with Dr Michael Rossi?

H15 What was the name of the school in *Fame*?

Guess the Drama Shows

Mixed up in the anagrams below are some top-rated drama series. See if you can sort them out – we've given you a few clues to help.

1 BLIND SONG ON RUN: Hot stuff? It's a flaming good show!

2 U SEE IF THE LOO HOTT: The period drama that had it all sewn up.

3 LEO HIT NINE DEN: A salty tale from the Seventies.

4 LES WON THAT: The best-known all-American family.

5 THIN SEAT: A heavenly role for Roger Moore.

6 HE SENT GRAVE: The Sixties team who fought for justice.

7 U MINK GOAT: The series ruled by Queenie.

8 IF MAN EVER SHONE PEN: Money from on high?

9 GIN IS RAW PONG: It's tough getting older for Ray Brooks.

10 RONNY, I RAVE PEACE: Taking time out in France.

11 CALL REGULAR MEN – R DATA'S STALE: The series with a lot of animal magic.

12 HA, DEER PIE STEW ENUF: The foundations were strong – in Germany, at least.

13 TA, MICE ON DATE: A drama with a *May to December* theme.

14 O WE STAR FOR FUN: Lucky battles in this £6-million series?

15 YES, ALE CROP IS LIFE: One of the best secret agents in the business.

Drama Wordsearch

How well up are you on the classic dramas? Put your knowledge to the test with the following questions – the answers can all be found in the wordsearch.

1 Name the actor who played Jesus of Nazareth (6,6)
2 Where in London was *Upstairs, Downstairs* set? (5,5)
3 Who wrote *Brideshead Revisited*? (6,5)
4 In which country was *The Jewel in the Crown* set? (5)
5 Who starred as Edward the Seventh? (7,4)
6 What was the first name of the patriach in *The Forsyte Saga*? (6)
7 Which movie heart-throb played a Southern gentleman in *North and South*? (7,6)
8 Who wrote the slave saga *Roots*? (4,5)
9 What was Peter Manson's job in *A Bouquet of Barbed Wire*? (9)
10 What was the name of Patrick Macnee's character in *The Avengers*? (4,5)
11 Which *Rock Follies* star went on to marry Dennis Waterman? (4,6)
12 What is the name of the club where Arthur Daley drinks? (3,10)
13 Who was the Waltons' oldest son? (4,3)
14 What was the name of the BBC drama about World War I flying aces? (5)
15 Name the hotel run by the Duchess of Duke Street (3,9)

O	T	R	U	L	A	L	E	N	S	K	A
E	H	R	L	E	I	O	S	A	N	T	O
Z	E	Y	O	B	N	H	O	J	N	I	B
Y	C	E	L	I	D	R	A	S	P	M	R
A	A	C	N	E	I	R	M	A	A	O	E
W	V	A	E	O	A	D	E	L	B	T	T
S	E	L	V	R	A	E	S	E	N	H	S
K	N	P	E	T	R	E	R	X	P	Y	E
C	D	N	L	E	H	T	L	H	X	W	H
I	I	O	Y	D	P	S	L	A	P	E	C
R	S	T	N	O	R	N	O	L	C	S	N
T	H	A	W	P	O	H	R	E	C	T	I
A	E	E	A	H	M	O	A	Y	O	N	W
P	L	A	U	S	E	J	N	A	E	L	E
L	O	S	G	N	I	W	T	C	K	D	H
J	R	E	H	S	I	L	B	U	P	O	T

SUPERCOOKS

Television has been a recipe for success for many culinary experts. If you've got a taste for food shows, test out our questions and see if you're a whiz in the kitchen.

A1 Which husband and wife team spread a little Kitchen Magic in the Fifties?

A2 Who was Graham Kerr better known as?

A3 On which foodie programme would you find Oz Clarke?

A4 Which television cook was far flung in 1993?

A5 Who is the jolly Jamaican lady who used to cook up a treat on breakfast television?

A6 Tasty delights for Richard and Judy on *This Morning* from this lady.

A7 Who has mastered the art of cooking and celebrity snooping?

A8 Which Indian cook starred opposite Billie Whitelaw in *Firm Friends*?

A9 Which one-time *Clapperboard* presenter is now a real food and drink man?

A10 Sophie Grigson had two shows on television at the same time. What did they advise us to do to our greens?

A11 Which cook presented her summer collection in 1993?

A12 Who is known as the Crafty Cook?

A13 Who went on a cook's tour of France?

A14 Who served up lashings of memories in a series about cookery during the years of World War II?

A15 What is the title of the BBC1 sitcom about a manic cook? Who plays the cook and what is the name of his character?

TOP OF THE POPS

Are you Number One when it comes to music? Try our questions to chart your success.

A1 In which year was *Top of the Pops* first broadcast?

A2 Where did the first show come from and who presented it?

A3 Which dance troupe outraged Mary Whitehouse when they made their first appearance on *Top of the Pops* in 1967?

A4 Which Number One hit did the BBC ban from being played on the show in 1969?

A5 In the Eighties television chiefs refused to allow another chart topper on *Top of the Pops*. However, it got a second chance in 1993 when it became a hit again. Name the song and the group.

A6 Who first chaired *Juke Box Jury* back in 1959?

A7 Which DJ appeared on the first panel?

A8 Also on the first panel was a girl dubbed 'a typical teenager'. Name her and the children's show she went on to present.

A9 Which television personality revived *Juke Box Jury* in 1979?

A10 Which former boxer was a regular on *Six-Five Special*?

A11 Name the lady who introduced the acts.

A12 Which chirpy cockney made his début on the show?

A13 Which up-and-coming pop superstar was accused of 'smouldering on screen' in the 1958 show *Oh Boy!*?

A14 Name the ITV pop show fronted in 1958 by Marty Wilde.

A15 Which Sixties show promised 'the weekend starts here'?

B1 Who is Harry Webb better known as?

B2 Which Live Aid star is behind *The Big Breakfast*?

B3 Which Sixties favourite relit her fire with 'Take That' in 1993?

B4 Who is Reg Dwight better known as?

B5 What was Tom Jones' first Number One?

B6 Which show launched pop star David Cassidy on the road to fame?

B7 Who was The Monkees' frontman and in which soap did he appear in 1961?

B8 Whose hits clocked up a massive 110 weeks on the chart in 1956 alone?

B9 Which 'nutty' band spent more time on the chart in 1980 than any other act?

B10 Who is Gerry Dorsey better known as?

B11 What was Cilla Black's first hit and what number did it get to on the chart?

B12 What was the name of Madonna's controversial book?

B13 Who joined George Michael when he sang 'Don't Let the Sun Go Down on Me'?

B14 What was the 1980 follow-up single to David Bowie's 'Space Oddity'?

B15 What was the Beatles' first hit?

C1   What was the *M★A★S★H* theme tune that became a hit?

C2   Which rock star provided the soundtrack to the *Batman* movie starring Michael Keaton?

C3   Which television comedy pair had a hit with 'At the Palace' in 1963?

C4   Which artist provided the theme tune to the 1976 show *Sailor* and what was the name of the song?

C5   Who sang the theme tune to *Love Hurts* – and what role is he best known for?

C6   What was the title of the chart topper sung by *It Ain't Half Hot, Mum*'s Windsor Davies and Don Estelle?

C7   Which *EastEnders* star had a hit with 'Anyone Can Fall in Love'?

C8   Name the Neighbour who was in good voice when he put on a colourful coat.

C9   Who sings the theme tune to *Watching*?

C10 Which Beatles hit is featured at the beginning and end of *The Wonder Years*?

C11 What was the title of Terry Wogan's only hit – and what number did it get to on the chart?

C12 Which Led Zeppelin song did cartoon-crazy Rolf Harris have a hit with in 1993?

C13 Which cult comedy show spawned a hit when its stars teamed up with Cliff Richard in the early Eighties?

C14 What was the *Minder* theme tune that became a hit and who sang it?

C15 Which rock superstar caused a stir – and a quick switch to the commercial break – when he used a four-letter word at the US Grammy Awards in 1994?

Popagram

Hidden in the jumbled up words below are some of the rock world's most famous stars. See if you can sort them out.

1 JOLT ON HEN: This rocket man's a wizard at pinball.

2 EG, GRIM JACK: The guy who can jump in a flash.

3 TRAINER NUT: Would you like her to be your private dancer?

4 C RIF-RAF CHILD: Congratulations! He's forever a young one.

5 JIM, CAN SHE CLOAK?: Is he dangerous or just off the wall?

6 NAN, LINE OXEN: Who's that girl? A real angel.

7 O AND MAN: She's always in vogue.

8 JO AVON AND SON: Once he'd washed off his soap image, his singing career took centre stage.

9 HAM CLINK LUCK: Simply a colourful chap.

10 SILLY VERSE EP: A man who needed some tender loving.

11 MONO JETS: What's new? This rocker came back with a kiss.

12 O I NEW RED VEST: Signed, sealed, delivered – he's yours.

13 O BAWDI DIVE: A boy who keeps on swinging.

14 CARLY CAN PUT ME: From one of four, he was winging up on his own.

15 OR NICE AND SOON: Nothing compares to her.

Chart-Toppers Wordsearch

Are you a hit when it comes to the rock scene? Below are fifteen classic Number One records – but who sang them? You'll find the answers hidden in the wordsearch.

1 'All Shook Up' (5,7)
2 'Help!' (3,7)
3 'Do Ya Think I'm Sexy?' (3,7)
4 'Hot Love' (1,3)
5 'Take a Chance on Me' (4)
6 'Message in a Bottle' (3,6)
7 'Call Me' (7)
8 'Do They Know It's Christmas?' (4,3)
9 'Honky Tonk Woman' (3,7,6)
10 'I Don't Like Mondays' (3,8,4)
11 'Living Doll' (5,7)
12 'Bohemian Rhapsody' (5)
13 'Thriller' (7,7)
14 'I Will Always Love You' (7,7)
15 'A Million Love Songs' (4,4)

T	G	S	B	Q	U	E	E	N	T	J	T
E	S	E	L	T	A	E	B	E	H	T	H
L	C	N	O	R	A	L	O	W	E	N	E
V	L	O	N	O	M	J	F	H	P	O	B
I	I	T	D	D	D	L	O	I	O	S	O
S	F	S	I	S	C	L	E	T	L	K	O
P	F	G	E	T	R	E	X	N	I	C	M
R	R	N	N	E	C	P	D	E	C	A	T
E	I	I	D	W	X	V	I	Y	E	J	O
S	C	L	E	A	R	E	A	H	S	L	W
L	H	L	T	R	B	E	D	O	B	E	N
E	A	O	R	T	C	B	N	U	D	A	R
Y	R	R	A	H	B	L	A	S	E	H	A
A	D	E	R	E	P	N	B	T	O	C	T
T	A	H	T	E	K	A	T	O	O	I	S
B	A	T	A	L	O	R	A	N	D	M	E

THE BIG SCREEN

Are you an armchair film buff who knows that Batman is nothing to do with cricket and that it's Richard Attenborough – rather than brother David – who's wild about movies? Then it's hooray for Hollywood in this reel of movie questions.

A1   What unusual form of transport was used by E.T. and his young friends to elude police in *E.T. – The Extra-Terrestrial*?

A2   What was Bob Hoskins' trade in *Super Mario Bros*?

A3   Who is the mother in *The Addams Family*?

A4   Which 1985 film starred a DeLorean car?

A5   Robin Williams starred in a film as an inspirational teacher. What was the name of the secret association set up by some of his pupils?

A6   In which film did Madonna appear as a sultry singer?

A7   In which film did Robin Williams have to learn to fly and what was his character?

A8   What strange creature did the Avon lady discover?

A9   In which 1990 film was young Kevin accidentally abandoned by his parents?

A10 Who is Superman's alter ego and what is his girlfriend's name?

A11 Which actor was the voice of Kirstie Alley's baby in *Look Who's Talking*?

A12 Which actors paired up to become an unlikely set of twins?

A13 In *Amadeus*, actor Tom Hulce portrayed Mozart with a particularly distinctive sound trait. What was it?

A14 In the film *Big* how did the child become magically grown up?

A15 Which Western featured a song implying that the two heroes were in need of an umbrella?

B1 In which film did the villain threaten to cancel Christmas?

B2 On top of which famous building did Tom Hanks and Meg Ryan meet in *Sleepless in Seattle*?

B3 After quitting city life in *Baby Boom* what sort of business did Diane Keaton set up in the country?

B4 Which film was a change of habit for Whoopi Goldberg?

B5 When things went wrong in Jurassic Park, owner Richard Attenborough consoled himself with what food?

B6 In which film did Jack Nicholson play a character that sounded a lot of fun, but who was really a nasty piece of work?

B7 In *Death Becomes Her*, what did Meryl Streep have on back to front?

B8 Who provided the voice of the genie in Disney's cartoon *Aladdin*?

B9 Which film featured a mogwai?

B10 What was the giant figure at the end of *Ghostbusters* made of?

B11 In *Indiana Jones and the Last Crusade*, Sean Connery played the father of a dashing hero who was searching for what?

B12 In which film did Rick Moranis play an inventor with very tiny children?

B13 In which film was Demi Moore protected by her phantom lover and who played him?

B14 What sort of shop did Bob Hoskins own in *Mermaids*?

B15 In which film did Sid James assume a royal role?

C1 What was the murder weapon in *Basic Instinct*?

C2 Where was Freddie Krueger more than just a bad dream?

C3 In which film did Marlon Brando play the mad Colonel Kurtz?

C4 In which film did Robert De Niro star as psychopath Max Cady?

C5 In *Alien*, what do crew members go foolishly in search of knowing that a monster lurks?

C6 What did Glenn Close do to the family rabbit in *Fatal Attraction*?

C7 Gene Hackman won an Oscar for playing a drugbusting cop in which film?

C8 What does the nanny from hell booby-trap to shattering effect in *The Hand That Rocks the Cradle*?

C9 What did Robert Redford offer Woody Harrelson in *Indecent Proposal*?

C10 What was the film and who was the actor who promised 'I'll be back'?

C11 Which actress was rated ten out of ten by Dudley Moore?

C12 What was the name of the murderer being tracked down by Jodie Foster in *The Silence of the Lambs*?

C13 Who played the Godfather?

C14 In *Misery*, what does Kathy Bates bring her captive James Caan to mark the completion of his novel?

C15 What film caused a sensation over its explicitness and led to its young star actress being described as the Sinner from Pinner?

D1 In which film did Marilyn Monroe sing 'Diamonds are a Girl's Best Friend'?

D2 Name Clint Eastwood's first spaghetti Western.

D3 Name the film in which Humphrey Bogart won an Oscar for his portrayal of a riverboat captain.

D4 In which film did the character Holly Golightly appear?

D5 Which film featured the Deadwood stagecoach?

D6 What was the name of Humphrey Bogart's detective in *The Maltese Falcon*?

D7 Who played Tarzan in the 1930s?

D8 A 1950 Bette Davis film became the most Oscar-nominated movie in history. What was it?

D9 Which veteran French charmer thanked 'eaven for little girls?

D10 Name James Stewart's six-foot white rabbit friend.

D11 Who played Frankenstein in the 1931 film?

D12 Which film featured World War II's bouncing bomb?

D13 Who was the medic played by Dirk Bogarde in the Doctor series of comedies and which glamorous French actress appeared in *Doctor at Sea*?

D14 Who didn't give a damn and in which film?

D15 Name the actors who formed the original Magnificent Seven.

E1 What was John Cleese's profession in *A Fish Called Wanda*?

E2 What musical instrument did Alan Rickman play in *Truly Madly Deeply*?

E3 What animal was the centre of attention in *A Private Function*?

E4 Who were the journalists played by Dustin Hoffman and Robert Redford in *All the President's Men*?

E5 Who went *Dirty Dancing*?

E6 Which 1991 film had a title track which became the longest-running Number One in the history of the British music charts? What was the song called and who sang it?

E7 Who went for the burn as a space maiden?

E8 What was the first James Bond movie and when was it released?

E9 How did Dustin Hoffman escape with his bride at the end of *The Graduate*?

E10 Which film told the story of Pu Yi?

E11 In which film does Tom Cruise play a smart lawyer who finds himself working for the Mafia?

E12 Who played a *Funny Girl*?

E13 For which Oscar-winning film did Nigel Havers put on his running shorts?

E14 Who is the object of Cyrano de Bergerac's passion?

E15 Which film featured Bing Crosby singing 'White Christmas'?

F1 In *Death Becomes Her*, what made Goldie Hawn resemble a Polo mint?

F2 Gerard Depardieu enters into a marriage of convenience with Andie MacDowell in *Green Card*. What is her job?

F3   Which film featured the entertaining Sally Bowles?

F4   What was Odd Job's lethal weapon in *Goldfinger*?

F5   In which film did Michelle Pfeiffer play a devout wife who was cruelly tricked by a French rake?

F6   In which film would you hear 'Who you gonna call?'

F7   Who was the fugitive played by Harrison Ford?

F8   What was the distinguishing feature of the real murderer in *The Fugitive*?

F9   The Addams Family pet is called Thing. What is it?

F10 Where were fried green tomatoes on the menu?

F11 For which political role did Ben Kingsley win an Oscar?

F12 What did Barbara Windsor lose when attempting a keep-fit session in *Carry on Camping*?

F13 Who played a crazy radio DJ working in a war zone and what was the film?

F14 How did the assassin disguise his gun in *The Bodyguard*?

F15 Which film is often described as 'the greatest ever made'?

The Big Screen Crossword

Across

5 Hollywood's glittering prize (5)

8 Ah, Jim Lad, this film featured an island for gold-diggers (8)

9 Michael Redgrave starred in this 1947 British movie *Fame is the* — (4)

10 Fire-power with Leslie Nielsen's bare-faced cheek produced a lot of laughs (5,3)

11 Really, they weren't just madly deeply in love (5)

14 Kenneth Branagh and Emma Thompson made a lot of fuss about nothing in this Shakespeare movie (3)

16 Richard Attenborough's epic movie about the Indian leader (6)

17 Miss Durbin, screen star of the Thirties and Forties (6)

18 Cross about the crazy crazy world? (3)

20 Ray Brooks had this special form of talent in Richard Lester's Sixties film (5)

24 Tough-guy actor who was a knockout in the ring (8)

25 Dead keen on animal life – like Dracula perhaps? (4)

26 The battle at the OK Corral (8)

27 Could be sharp, rather like the runner in the cult movie starring Harrison Ford (5)

Down

1 Robert Redford and Paul Newman teamed up for a movie with a perhaps painful twist in the tail (5)

2 Michael Douglas won an Oscar for his portrayal of this 'greed is good' character (5)

3 Theatrical way of describing how an actor speaks straight to camera . . . Certainly not in the middle! (5)

4 David Niven went in this global direction in eighty days (6)

6 The chap who wore his knickers on top of his tights, but still managed to save the world (8)

7 High altitude laughs in this disaster spoof (8)

12 Hannibal Lecter had the taste for being one of these (8)

13 Thanks to her tutor Michael Caine, Rita became this (8)

14 Robin Hood had to be sure of this to hit his target (3)

15 Jack Lemmon and Walter Matthau formed this unusual couple (3)

19 Dudley Moore starred in this film about a millionaire with girl trouble (6)

21 He had a summer holiday and a wonderful life (5)

22 A city you couldn't miss in Western starring Errol Flynn (5)

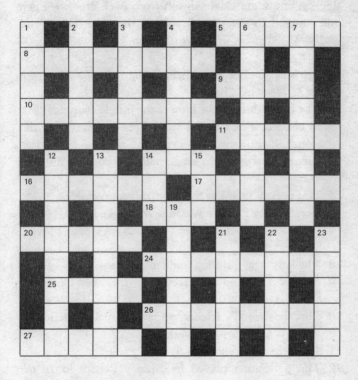

23 First name of the legendary
actress who knew all about
baby Jane (5)

The Big Screen Wordsearch

Reckon you know Mel Gibson from Mel Brooks? Then put yourself to the test by solving the clues below and finding the answers in the wordsearch.

1 Christopher Lee played this villain in *The Man with the Golden Gun* (10)
2 The bear who was the king of the jungle swingers (5)
3 Michael J. Fox's career took flight as Marty —, the teenager who went *Back to the Future* (5)
4 Screen horror with an appalling taste in humans (8,6)
5 You must remember this pianist from *Casablanca* (3)
6 Recall Dirty Harry's surname and make his day! (8)
7 Kathleen Turner was the voice behind Roger's lovely ladyfriend (7)
8 The lady who put the Graduate in a jam? (3,8)
9 As this dedicated cop, Kevin Costner was Untouchable (5,4)
10 Clint Eastwood's friend had real animal attraction in *Every Which Way but Loose* (5)
11 The *Star Wars* villain (5,5)
12 The policeman played by Sidney Poitier in *In the Heat of the Night* (6,5)
13 He's butler to the Addams family (5)
14 He may have looked like a nice boy – but he was a little devil (6)
15 The creepy motel owner from *Psycho* (6,5)
16 She was the girl John Travolta wanted in *Grease* (5)
17 The flower-seller who Professor Higgins transformed into a fair lady (5,9)

O	M	A	S	A	J	R	E	T	C	E	L
E	O	A	S	M	C	E	B	R	O	T	A
L	M	L	M	S	A	I	S	M	F	Y	B
T	D	N	A	B	E	K	S	S	M	L	I
T	V	A	I	B	R	N	E	G	I	F	N
I	D	H	R	I	L	O	T	J	E	C	N
L	S	A	L	T	Y	W	A	O	S	M	A
O	E	L	M	L	H	C	B	D	I	G	H
O	M	L	O	I	P	V	N	J	N	L	X
D	S	A	U	G	E	B	A	A	C	H	E
A	Y	C	P	R	Q	N	M	D	U	W	E
Z	A	D	E	I	C	A	R	O	E	D	P
I	S	A	N	V	R	H	O	M	Y	R	O
L	I	W	X	A	P	T	N	L	E	S	K
E	M	S	C	I	S	P	C	T	J	B	G
M	R	S	R	O	B	I	N	S	O	N	A

18 'I'll be back,' said Arnold Schwarzenegger and sure enough he was – he recreated his role as this android in a sequel (2,1)

59

NAME GAME

What's in a name? Listed below are television characters who are all better known by their surnames. Can you remember their first names?

A1 Sergeant Lewis from *Morse*.

A2 Kojak.

A3 Fletcher in *Porridge*.

A4 Pop Larkin from *The Darling Buds of May*.

A5 Wicksy (Wicks) in *EastEnders*.

A6 Bilko.

A7 Cannon.

A8 Starsky and Hutch.

A9 Dempsey and Makepeace.

A10 Ironside.

A11 Shelley.

A12 Duffy from *Casualty*

A13 Detective Constable Lines from *The Bill*.

A14 Shoestring.

A15 Dr Finlay.

A16 Maigret.

A17 Callan.

A18 Poirot.

A19 Van der Valk.

A20 Wexford.

GAME SHOWS

You either love 'em or hate 'em – but there's no escaping the game show presenters. How well do you know them?

A1 Which ex *Game for a Laugh* host went *Going for Gold*?

A2 'You'll like this' – name the game show and the magical host.

A3 Which town did *The Sale of the Century* come from?

A4 Which Generation girl did Bruce Forsyth meet at a Miss Longest Legs contest?

A5 Who took over *The Generation Game* from Brucie and who was his right-hand girl?

A6 Which former *Golden Shot* girl is the mother of pop star Chesney Hawkes?

A7 Which year saw the start of *Opportunity Knocks* and who was the original host?

A8 Who revived the show in later years?

A9 Who was the host of the Fifties game show *The 64,000 Question*?

A10 Which show was the forerunner of *Name That Tune*?

A11 What did Jim Bowen do for a living before fronting *Bullseye*?

A12 On which game show does Mr Chips play a starring role?

A13 What did all the contestants on *Blankety Blank* go home with?

A14 Which Japanese game show is more like a form of torture for its contestants?

A15 What were the names of the two outrageously camp game shows hosted by Julian Clary?

Game for a Laugh?

A whole host of game show presenters past and present are hidden in the anagrams below. How long will it take you to work them out?

1 ROY'S BUTCH REF: It's always nice to see him.
2 BUN'S HOME BOOK: A square sort of celebrity.
3 BLOBS SHONE: A blockbusting star.
4 I NEAR A NECK: There's no need to hunt for this treasure.
5 CHART R TRAINS: The main man who can easily lose a million.
6 LONDON DEEMS: A real TV addict.
7 BRON RUNS DOG: A high factor sort of guy.
8 DEAR CRIME LADY H: Game shows are murder for this host.
9 EE, I SMALL CHAP: Give us a clue to this man's identity.
10 Y HER KNELLY?: A golden wonder.
11 A BALL CLICK: The lady who makes a match.
12 ME WIN JOB: Get right on target with this chap.
13 SALES DOWN: He was the man who never went blank when it came to a joke.
14 O, THERE'S LIL CREW: He'd come down if the money was OK.
15 C MP IN YELL BACK: A host in a real spin.

Game Show Wordsearch

Are you game for a quiz on game shows? The answers to the following questions are all hidden in the wordsearch. See if you can find them.

1 Which Radio Two DJ went *Blankety Blank*? (5,5)
2 Who was Ted Rogers' trusty metal sidekick? (5,3)
3 Which comedian took over *The Generation Game* for a spell? (5,7)
4 Who is the *Wheel of Fortune* hostess? (5,7)
5 What sport is featured in Jim Davidson's *Big Break*? (7)
6 Who was the original 'quiz inquisitor' on *Take Your Pick*? (7,5)
7 What was the name of the prize-winning round on *Blockbusters*? (3,4,3)
8 Which show teams Roy Walker with Mr Chips? (11)
9 Every one of these counts for Paul Daniels (6)
10 Who supplied the bolt in *The Golden Shot*? (6)
11 How many stars appear in *Celebrity Squares*? (4)
12 Who hosted *The Sale of the Century*? (8,7)
13 What did Tom O'Connor ask contestants to name? (4)
14 Which singer presented *Family Fortunes*? (3,8)
15 On which show do contestants have to avoid the hot-spots? (6,2,5)

A	C	N	T	B	R	L	G	S	O	S	N
M	A	O	M	E	T	L	D	E	P	T	I
I	T	S	A	R	H	E	S	C	T	R	C
C	C	Y	X	N	E	R	P	O	E	I	H
H	H	A	B	I	G	E	N	N	R	K	O
A	P	R	Y	E	O	L	I	D	R	E	L
E	H	G	G	X	L	N	C	P	Y	I	A
L	R	Y	R	R	D	R	D	S	W	T	S
M	A	R	A	E	R	E	T	O	O	L	P
I	S	R	V	P	U	K	U	L	G	U	A
L	E	A	E	A	N	O	N	C	A	C	R
E	N	L	S	D	D	O	E	N	N	K	S
S	C	E	R	L	F	N	S	P	O	Y	O
O	R	N	O	D	U	S	T	Y	B	I	N
A	P	O	L	O	N	E	R	P	C	D	S
C	A	R	O	L	S	M	I	L	L	I	E

OUT OF THIS WORLD

If you're gripped by creatures from another planet and the wonders of time travel then test your skill with this galaxy of sci-fi questions.

A1 In which year was *Doctor Who* first shown?

A2 What was the name of the Doctor's granddaughter?

A3 What does TARDIS stand for?

A4 Who played the first Doctor?

A5 Which Doctor went on to become a Medic?

A6 Which Doctor later acquired a turnip as a head?

A7 What is the Doctor's home planet?

A8 What was the BBC's first sci-fi series that shocked the nation in 1953?

A9 Who was the chief navigator in *Star Trek*?

A10 Which crew member did Captain Kirk always ask to return him to the spaceship and what was his job title?

A11 Who was Lou Ferrigno better known as?

A12 In which show would you find the spaceship Liberator?

A13 In *The Man from UNCLE*, where were the organizers' headquarters?

A14 Who played Ilya Kuryakin?

A15 What did UNCLE stand for?

B1 Who was the Invisible Man's sister?

B2 What was Batman's real name and who played him on TV?

B3   In which city did he and Robin fight crime?

B4   Who played his arch-villain Penguin?

B5   On what sort of vehicle was *Stingray* set?

B6   What was the name of the organization featured in *Thunderbirds*?

B7   Who was their arch-enemy?

B8   Which member of the team drove a pink Rolls-Royce?

B9   What was its registration number?

B10 Which series featured a character named Dr Spencer Quist?

B11 What was the name of the series that portrayed Britain after a deadly world-wide plague?

B12 In which show did the organization Nemesis feature?

B13 Who devised, produced and starred in *The Prisoner*?

B14 What was the number of the Prisoner's chief adversary?

B15 Where was the show filmed?

Sci-Fi Wordsearch

Do sci-fi shows send you into orbit? Put yourself to the test with the following questions – all the answers can be found in the wordsearch.

1 What colour was the Incredible Hulk? (5)
2 Which big movie star played Mork from Ork? (5,8)
3 What was the name of the spaceship in *Star Trek*? (3,10)
4 Which show features Scott Bakula and Dean Stockwell? (7,4)
5 Who was the Six Million Dollar Man? (3,6)
6 Who pilots Thunderbird One? (5,5)
7 Which sci-fi show did *Emmerdale*'s Frazer Hines appear in? (6,3)
8 Who was Captain Kirk's half-Vulcan first officer? (2,5)
9 Name Doctor Who's arch-enemies. (6)
10 Which man was behind *Stingray* and *Thunderbirds*? (5,8)
11 What was the name of the hero in *Stingray*? (4,7)
12 What was the name of Robert Vaughn's character in *The Man from UNCLE*? (8,4)
13 Who was the scientist who became the Invisible Man? (2,5,5)
14 Who took over the female role when Honor Blackman left *The Avengers*? (5,4)
15 A webbed-fingered Patrick Duffy became the man from this place. (8)

D	R	P	E	T	E	R	B	R	A	D	Y
A	T	R	E	P	O	G	N	P	U	N	C
N	L	A	D	A	L	E	K	S	S	A	L
S	M	O	R	E	Q	R	R	D	S	P	E
R	N	O	A	Y	U	R	O	R	E	O	E
P	P	S	T	C	A	Y	B	E	N	L	M
G	G	I	R	A	N	A	I	D	T	E	A
A	R	E	O	R	T	N	N	O	E	O	J
T	E	B	Y	T	U	D	W	C	R	N	O
L	E	R	T	T	M	E	I	T	P	S	R
A	N	O	E	T	L	R	L	O	R	O	S
N	E	N	M	O	E	S	L	R	I	L	O
T	O	R	P	C	A	O	I	W	S	O	L
I	A	N	E	S	P	N	A	H	E	R	D
S	C	P	S	L	P	A	M	O	E	N	E
R	E	X	T	D	M	R	S	P	O	C	K

THE SOAPS

They're top of the television ratings – so if you love your *Neighbours* from *EastEnders* to *Emmerdale*, then these questions are right up your Street!

Coronation Street

A1 What were the names of Ena Sharples' two companions who used to sit with her in the Rovers' snug?

A2 Pat Phoenix as Elsie Tanner was called 'the sexiest woman on TV' by which former Prime Minister?

A3 Which character died on screen of a heart attack in the Rovers' snug?

A4 Which Professional chap played the leader of a hippy commune squatting at Number Eleven back in the Sixties?

A5 Why did Hilda Ogden fly out to Australia in 1970?

A6 How did Ken Barlow's wife Val die?

A7 Emily made a leap year proposal in 1964 only to jilt her intended at the altar. Name the character who lost out and the actor who played him.

A8 How did Emily's husband Ernie Bishop die?

A9 What went wrong when Stan Ogden thought he'd had a big win on the pools?

A10 How did Alan Bradley meet a sticky end?

A11 Where did Bet flee to when the Rovers became too much and what was she working as when Alec found her?

A12 Who rescued Bet when the Rovers went up in flames?

A13 How did Derek manage to cause a flood in The Kabin?

A14 How did Maureen console herself when she called off her marriage to Reg after finding him in a compromising position with another woman?

A15 How did Derek try to make out that aliens had landed in Des's garden?

Brookside

B1   What did Paul Collins find had been stolen when he moved into his house on Brookside Close?

B2   Who played the wacky computer programmer Alan Partridge and in which other soap did he go on to have a regular role?

B3   Who was really Barry Grant's father?

B4   Where did Petra commit suicide?

B5   Who was the villain Barry and Terry had dodgy dealings with?

B6   Who stood bail for George Jackson when he was arrested after a warehouse raid?

B7   What was the name of the teacher Tracy Corkhill had an affair with?

B8   How did Sinbad propose to Marcia?

B9   How did the Close find out that Gordon was gay?

B10 What was the guilty secret of Heather's second husband Nick?

B11 How did Damon Grant die?

B12 What was the name of the car dealer Annabelle Collins had a fling with?

B13 Who rescued Jackie Dixon when she was trapped in a blazing classroom?

B14 What is the name of Max's first wife and his two children?

B15 What is the name of the nightclub Barry Grant runs?

Emmerdale

C1   Whose death did *Emmerdale* start with in 1972?

C2   What was the title of Jack Sugden's best-selling novel?

C3   What were the names of the twins Peggy Skilbeck gave birth to just three months before her death?

C4   What was Clive Hinton arrested for when he went to visit his clergyman father in Athens?

C5   What did Tom Merrick receive a suspended sentence for at the end of 1981?

C6   Why did Beckindale lose its chance of winning the best-kept village title in 1983?

C7   Who discovered Sam Pearson's body when he died in his sleep?

C8   Who eventually confessed to killing Harry Mowlem?

C9   What was the name of Dolly Skilbeck's illegitimate son, who played him and which soap character is he now best known as?

C10 Why was Jack Sugden jailed for contempt of court?

C11 How did Dennis Rigg meet his end?

C12 To whom did Lorraine Nelson reveal her incest nightmare?

C13 Which soap supremo was brought in by *Emmerdale* bosses to mastermind the Lockerbie-style air disaster?

C14 Who found Chris Tate when he was trapped by rubble after the plane crash?

C15 What was Shirley Turner's disreputable former job?

Dallas and Dynasty

D1 What was the name of the ranch where the Ewing clan lived?

D2 Where did Bobby and Pam meet – and where did they marry?

D3 What did JR's car registration plate read?

D4 Who was first arrested for shooting JR and who was eventually found guilty?

D5 Who is Pam Ewing's father?

D6 How did Jack Ewing meet his end?

D7 What was the name of the Southern belle JR married?

D8 What was the name of the diner Lucy Ewing took a job in?

D9 Who was Jock Ewing's illegitimate son?

D10 What was the name of the adventurer Pam Ewing fell for?

D11 What was Krystle's job title when she worked for Blake in *Dynasty*?

D12 In which city was *Dynasty* set?

D13 Who was Fallon found naked with in the swimming pool?

D14 What caused Krystle to miscarry?

D15 Who was Alexis accused of murdering and who was eventually found to be the killer?

Neighbours

E1 Which Neighbour was married to a killer?

E2 Name Madge's children.

E3 Who came close to making a suicide attempt by leaping off a bridge?

E4 Who disappeared from the top of a cliff?

E5 Name the twins who both became romantically involved with Paul.

E6 When Todd died in a car crash he was in a hurry to reach Phoebe. Why?

E7 Who did Doug Willis have a fling with?

E8 What did Stephen give Phoebe for her eighteenth birthday?

E9 What did Debbie and Rick give leukaemia sufferer Terry?

E10 What were Beth and Hannah looking for when they went to the old cottage behind Lassiter's and became trapped in a blaze?

E11 How did Michael attempt to kill Julie Martin in the garden?

E12 What was the cause of Jim Robinson's death?

E13 Who persuaded a friend to turn into her lover?

E14 What was the name of Toby Mangel's dog?

E15 Who was the actor who quit Ramsay Street to become a schoolteacher in Summer Bay?

Home and Away

F1   Why did Pippa and Tom Fletcher decide to foster children?

F2   Who jilted Frank at the altar and why?

F3   Who developed a drink problem after she was brutally attacked?

F4   Who married a sheep farmer?

F5   Where did Meg die and what was the cause of her death?

F6   Who were Bobby's real parents?

F7   Who raised eyebrows by having an affair with an older woman?

F8   Who attempted to blackmail Fisher about the accidental killing of Shane Wilson?

F9   Why did Roxy become the subject of a blackmail attempt?

F10   Why did Shane go on the run from the police?

F11   How did David die?

F12   How did Bobby die?

F13   What was the name of Sophie's baby and who was the father?

F14   What was the name of Pippa's baby and how did he die?

F15   What did Sam do to Adam when he learnt he was responsible for Bobby's death?

EastEnders

G1   What is the fictional London borough in which *EastEnders* is set?

G2   Who was the father of Michelle's child?

G3   Who made a suicide attempt by washing down sleeping pills with alcohol?

G4   Who got married just before dying?

G5   Where did Ricky Butcher and Sam Mitchell elope to?

G6   Who set fire to the Queen Vic?

G7   Why did Pat Butcher end up behind bars?

G8   Why did Phil Mitchell marry Nadia?

G9   What distressing event caused Michelle to make an emotional television appeal?

G10 What shattered Aidan's dreams of becoming a professional footballer?

G11 How did Pete Beale die?

G12 Who was the woman that Arthur Fowler had a fling with?

G13 What marred the birth of Cindy and Ian Beale's twins?

G14 How did nasty Nick Cotton once attempt to murder Dot?

G15 Who was murdered by being stabbed through the heart?

The Soaps Crossword

Are you a soap fan? Put yourself to the test with our super soap crossword.

Across

1 The Neighbour who's surf crazy (4)

2 He was the man behind *EastEnders*' Frank (4,4)

7 She serves up a treat in the *Home and Away* diner (5)

9 The country Frank headed for when he quit Summer Bay (7)

11 A man who's hard to track down – *Brookside*'s Barry Grant is this sort of character (7)

12 Fear of this causing an explosion resulted in an evacuation of Coronation Street back in 1961 (3)

13 The hot sort of affairs *Dynasty*'s Alexis enjoyed (6)

15 Take no notice of – like Peter Harrison tried to do when Jimmy Corkhill began harassing him in *Brookside* (6)

17 The Street's hairnet-clad harridan (3)

19 She's better known as Albert Square's Sharon (7)

23 *Neighbours*' Helen, the lady everyone turns to in a crisis (7)

24 One-time *EastEnders* landlady – or the Street girl who left for Mexico (5)

25 It's where the Albert Square locals enjoy a little liquid refreshment (5,3)

26 Stan Ogden liked a string one! (4)

Down

1 The ruler of *Dynasty* – or one of the Summer Bay old boys (5)

3 First name of *Take the High Road*'s one-time post mistress (6)

4 The time of day when the Rovers fills up (7)

5 The family in charge in *Dallas* (5)

6 Often driven by Don down Coronation Street (4)

8 Madge left him behind in Ramsay Street (3)

10 The Street's Terry and Lisa walked down this – before Terry did a runner later that day! (5)

13 The fast actress behind Annie Walker (5)

14 Reg Holdsworth's blushing bride (7)

16 The name Ramsay Street's Marco and Rick share (6)

18 From Sugden to Kempinski – she's *Emmerdale*'s matriarch (5)

20 The vehicle that put an end to
   the Street's nasty Alan
   Bradley (4)
21 The *Home and Away* bad boy
   who fell for Sarah (3)
22 A Russian double one was sent
   to *Take the High Road*'s Sir
   John for vetting (5)

The Soaps Wordsearch

The following characters are familiar names from the soaps – there are three each from *Coronation Street*, *EastEnders*, *Brookside*, *Emmerdale*, *Home and Away*, *Neighbours* and *Dallas*. But how well do you know them? See if you can spot their surnames in the wordsearch.

Curly	Ron	Greg
Rita	Jackie	Lou
Reg	Jack	Dorothy
Pauline	Archie	Toby
Grant	Seth	Bobby
Clive	Ailsa	Clayton
Frank	Pippa	Ray

M	H	O	L	D	S	W	O	R	T	H	F
A	E	R	D	G	N	I	W	E	L	G	C
R	O	M	I	T	C	H	E	L	L	F	O
M	L	P	E	A	R	N	T	W	A	A	R
S	J	O	F	V	O	R	C	O	H	R	K
T	R	O	G	E	R	S	D	F	S	L	H
R	L	R	D	R	A	B	C	H	R	O	I
O	S	E	I	N	S	B	A	F	A	W	L
N	R	S	X	I	U	E	R	K	M	R	L
G	P	D	O	E	L	R	P	X	E	T	O
N	O	R	N	R	L	K	E	K	R	U	B
A	S	E	T	E	I	O	N	E	S	A	R
M	T	C	G	A	V	S	T	A	R	S	O
C	T	N	T	R	A	W	E	T	S	I	O
O	A	R	O	L	N	A	R	E	N	R	K
M	W	O	R	S	U	G	D	E	N	E	S

Soapagrams

Are you a real soap addict? See if you can work out which characters are hidden in the anagrams below – we've added a few clues to help you out.

1 SEND GREY CUP: A real busybody down the Street.

2 BITE GLORY: She'll always return to the Rovers.

3 TIM'S LOW VAIN: A Kabin girl who's all of a dither.

4 ROLF, R U THE WAR?: Dig this Albert Square regular.

5 HER PUT T'CAB: Driving was the downfall of this EastEnder.

6 A BY THE LAKE: She's an East End girl who fell for one of the brothers.

7 HE BIG MAD SOP: This lady was a great Neighbour.

8 I DIG SLOW, LU: But this Ramsay Street resident is a dab hand with a spade.

9 JIM CONS HONK: A Liverpool lad with a pizza the action.

10 I'M A FAR TRAIN CHAP: This *Brookside* girl gets the Max out of her life.

11 JUDE'S GONE: He was one of *Emmerdale*'s leading lights.

12 FAT RAT KEN: Countryman who's a farm favourite.

13 WE RING J: *Dallas*'s real baddie.

14 CALF BINS REF: An oily sort of character.

15 CORNY GREAT KILTS, RN: A sparkling gem of the *Dynasty* clan.

ADVENTURE

Are you an armchair adventurer? Take a trip through our wildlife and travel questions and see how you fare.

A1 In which country did Alan Whicker work as a war journalist?

A2 Which notorious leader did Whicker interview in 1968?

A3 Which husband and wife team presented the popular *On Safari* in 1958?

A4 What was the name of the show which had David Attenborough filming wild animals and bringing them back to Britain for London Zoo?

A5 Who was the underwater explorer who inspired singer John Denver to write a song about his work?

A6 What was the name of his boat?

A7 Which nature documentary series was made with 1.25 million feet of film shot in thirty different countries and had the crew travelling one and a half million miles in more than three years?

A8 In 1992 Michael Palin travelled from Pole to Pole. Which island did he first stop off at and how many countries did he visit altogether?

A9 One of Alan Whicker's shows featured an ultimate package tour costing £21,500 and lasting thirty-four days. But how many countries did he get to visit – was it ten, fourteen, thirty or thirty-four?

A10 Which 1974 science show launched the career of bearded botanist David Bellamy?

A11 Which long-running natural history series began in 1961 with a fifteen-minute piece on the wildlife of London?

A12 In which city is the BBC's history unit – the biggest of its kind in the world – based?

A13 Who were the German husband and wife team famed for their undersea programmes in the Fifties and Sixties?

A14 Name the BBC1 wildlife series presented by David Attenborough on the chilly mysteries of the Antarctic.

A15 Who was the actor who left behind his usual role of fighting the villains to spy on wolves for a wildlife special?

TELEVISION BUFF'S CHALLENGE

So you reckon you're a bit of an expert on what's on the box? Then put on your thinking cap and try this lucky dip of questions, which include some real testers for your memory.

A1 He played a Blott on the Landscape – but this actor is best known as which screen detective?

A2 Which series featured Collier and Ferris?

A3 Which bone did Liza break in *Second Thoughts*?

A4 If the broken bone did not mend properly what did she fear could be the consequence?

A5 Name the mother in the Australian fly-on-the-wall documentary series *Sylvania Waters*.

A6 Which Western featured the Ponderosa ranch?

A7 In which television Western did Clint Eastwood star?

A8 What is the link between *Dallas* and a man with webbed fingers and toes?

A9 What character did Danniella Westbrook play in *EastEnders*?

A10 Who blasted Brad Willis with a shotgun in *Neighbours*?

A11 *Coronation Street*'s Raquel went off to a modelling school. What was it called and where was it?

A12 John Drake was the main character in which series?

A13 In *Keeping Up Appearances* what is the name of Daisy's granddaughter?

A14 Who is Daisy's husband, what does he never wear and what does he have on each arm?

A15 In *Keeping Up Appearances*, who lives at 23 Blossom Avenue?

B1 What is the name of Del's business in *Only Fools and Horses*?

B2 Name the local gangster, his wife and his dozy sidekick.

B3 Who moved into Del's life and what did they name their son?

B4 Name the charity organization that Tessa worked for in *Love Hurts*.

B5 Where did Tessa and Frank get married?

B6 What connects *Love Hurts* with a chirpy little bird?

B7 Who was Nora Batty's husband in *Last of the Summer Wine* and what was his passion in life?

B8 Apart from Nora, what is Compo's passion in life?

B9 When Victor Meldrew took up a job as a hotel doorman why did it turn out to be a hair-raising experience?

B10 When the Meldrews found themselves looking after a baby, why was the child entranced by a garden gnome?

B11 What caused Victor to crawl on his holiday?

B12 Name Tom's son and daughter-in-law in *Waiting for God*.

B13 What event in hospital caused Diana to need oxygen?

B14 Stephanie Cole, who plays Diana, starred as a doctor in which series?

B15 Name Dame Edna Everage's long-suffering bridesmaid.

C1 Name the actor who played a big-screen man-eater and then faced man-eaters himself in a television wildlife special.

C2 In *Coronation Street* what happened to Derek when he organized a theatre trip to London?

C3 In *Brookside*, where did the Jordache family hide Trevor's body?

C4 Where did Phoebe from *Neighbours* plan to give birth to her baby?

C5 What was the name of the development in Spain where the ex-pats in *Eldorado* lived?

C6 What was the name of the series starring Bill Nighy as a philandering academic?

C7 Known for more glamorous roles, Shirley Anne Field played a dowdy nurse in which controversial series?

C8 Who was terrified of his fearsome Aunt Agatha?

C9 He's rubber, grey and partial to peas. Who is he and what is the programme in which he appears like this?

C10 In *Open All Hours*, who was the nurse that Arkwright was passionate about?

C11 In a comedy-drama special, Rik Mayall played a reluctant bridegroom who woke up on a train missing part of his clothing and with something strapped to his head. What was on his head and what was missing?

C12 Name the Bond girl who became a medical expert way out west.

C13 How did Richard Briers suffer brain damage in *If You See God, Tell Him*?

C14 What was the name of Richard Briers' character and that of his wife in *Ever Decreasing Circles*?

C15 Their friends were a devoted couple along the road. Who were they?

D1 Which comedian had a big hit with 'Dizzy'?

D2 Which outsize spotty star had an outsize Christmas hit?

D3 Cobra and Shadow starred in which all-action show?

D4 Fairfax and Carstairs were jolly good chaps on the run from the Germans in which long-running show?

D5 Sooty made headline news in November 1993. What was the story – later denied by Matthew Corbett – that caused the storm?

D6 Which television detective tried to propose to the love of his life while clutching a bunch of red roses at Waterloo Station?

D7 How many years did *Z Cars* run?

D8 What is the connection between *Z Cars* and *Chariots of Fire*?

D9 In the final series of *The Professionals*, how did Doyle nearly die?

D10 What is the connection between the crime series *Shoestring* and *Casualty*?

D11 Which *Coronation Street* star played Detective Sergeant Russell in the police series *No Hiding Place*?

D12 Who is Maigret's wife and what particular skill of hers is he a great admirer of?

D13 What dangerous drug was Sherlock Holmes addicted to?

D14 Who is the British singer who made the big time

and went on to have a screen romance with Don Johnson in *Miami Vice*?

D15   What is the link between *Bedknobs and Broomsticks* and a crime-busting authoress?

E1   Who is the former football star who should know when it's going to rain?

E2   Who was the footballer who showed off his language skills when he played himself in a television drama series?

E3   Who was the Manageress?

E4   Who was the actor who starred in both *The Manageress* and *All in the Game*?

E5   Who were *The Two of Us*?

E6   Name the show in which Prunella Scales played a widow called Sarah.

E7   What does the audience shout out when Dame Edna instructs Madge to investigate the bedrooms in her *Neighbourhood Watch*?

E8   What was ATV replaced by in January 1982?

E9   Joan Collins and Pauline Collins both starred in an episode of which twist in the tale series?

E10   In *EastEnders*, what did Pauline hit Arthur with when he told her he was having an affair?

E11   What did Don do to frighten hairdresser Denise in *Coronation Street*?

E12   When Julie Martin stood for the Erinsborough council elections in *Neighbours*, how many votes did she get?

E13   Which soap star was part of a rock band called Check 1–2 and scored an Australian award for a chart-topping version of 'Mona'?

E14 Which soap star was a hit in a loin-cloth?

E15 A comedy actor had a Number One hit in 1970 with a record about a close relative. What was the record called and who sang it?

F1 Sam Kelly who played *'Allo 'Allo*'s Captain Hans Geering received a huge promotion to play which role in the prisoner-of-war camp spoof *Stalag Luft*?

F2 Which Oscar-winner won an Emmy for his portrayal of Hitler?

F3 Who was the Python who went on to make a television series in which he appeared naked and covered in mud?

F4 Name the series that featured the downfall of romantic novelist Mary Fischer.

F5 Who starred as sheet-music salesman Arthur Parker and what was the series?

F6 Which series concerned the discrediting of the British Royal Family by a corrupt Prime Minister?

F7 What is the name of Dorien's husband in *Birds of a Feather*?

F8 Name the BBC costume drama that included Ma Larkin actress Pam Ferris in the cast.

F9 Name the drama series that featured the love affair between Daphne Manners and Hari Kumar.

F10 Who was the leader of the pirates on the Black Pig?

F11 How old was Adrian Mole when he wrote his diary?

F12 Who caused a titter or two as Lurcio in ancient Rome?

F13 He wore a beret, raincoat and was married to Betty. Who was he?

F14 Who called his cat Vienna because 'if he sees another pair of eyes out there, then it's goodnight Vienna'.

F15 'And now for something completely different' was a catchphrase in which show?

1 This Captain Fantastic has also been a delivery boy, detective, market trader and a jack of all trades. Name the show he's in here – and the four others.

2 He may be best known as wheeler-dealer Mike Baldwin but there was life before *Coronation Street*. Name the Sixties detective series Johnny Briggs starred in.

3 Richard Briers has had a good life in sitcoms. But in the classic Seventies comedy about self-sufficiency what job did he give up to 'grow it' alone?

4 It's more than thirty years since this actor put on a school cap and cheeky grin to star in *Just William*. Who is he?

5 He's fronted a whole host of game shows, but what was the sitcom Bruce Forsyth starred in?

6 The hat's not quite up to tea with the vicar – and certainly not a candlelight supper. Who is the actress and what is her most famous role?

7 He's looking every inch the country gent in tie and tweeds, but nowadays he's more at home in T-shirt and jeans. Who is he and what role is he best known for?

8 The *Absolutely Fabulous* Joanna Lumley became a New Avenger in the Seventies. What was her role and what was it named after?

9 Will you be surprise, surprised when you realize who this is? Can you remember her first Number One record?

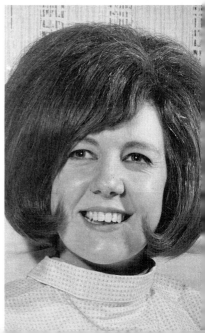

10 This young man went on to revive a show first hosted by Michael Miles. Who is he and what was the programme?

11 Frankie Howerd swapped his trousers for a toga in *Up Pompeii!*, but who did he play?

12 He's modelled knitting patterns, been a saint – he's even been James Bond. But Roger Moore once teamed up with a Hollywood star for a crime-busting series. Name the actor and the programme.

13 He's looking relaxed here but Lionel Blair was anything but laid back when his stage play fell apart in a television practical joke in 1994. Who was behind his embarrassment?

14 Joan Collins is best known as *Dynasty* queen Alexis. Everyone thought she would come to a sticky end in the final episode when she was pushed off a balcony with husband Dexter. How did she cheat death to return for *Dynasty: The Reunion*?

15 She's a nurse here but Lynda Bellingham has played three major 'mumsy' roles. Name them.

16 Sixties heart-throb Adam Faith was a hit as Frank Carver in *Love Hurts*. What was Frank's trade before he became a businessman and how did he really hit the big time in the third series?

17 This young chap went on to make a 'nice little earner' in films and television. Who is he?

ANSWERS

COMEDY

Vintage Comedy

A1 Godber
A2 Stanley
A3 *Going Straight*
A4 Walmington-on-Sea
A5 Bank manager
A6 Corporal
A7 Stupid Boy
A8 Silly Old Moo
A9 Rita; Una Stubbs
A10 Margo and Jerry Leadbetter
A11 Pinky and Perky
A12 Sybil
A13 Barcelona
A14 The war
A15 He gave his car a good thrashing with a fallen tree branch

B1 Audrey Fforbes-Hamilton
B2 Brabinger
B3 Grantleigh Manor
B4 Czech
B5 Grace Brothers
B6 Wendy Richard – she played Miss Brahms in *Are You Being Served?* and Pauline Fowler in *EastEnders*
B7 John Inman
B8 Ladies' lingerie
B9 Pauline Collins
B10 Sandra; Beryl
B11 Adam and Russell
B12 Dentist; *Fairly Secret Army*

B13 Ria; the car had a Union Jack painted on the roof
B14 *Nanny*
B15 *Joint Account*

C1 Sonia
C2 France
C3 *Bless This House*; Sid James
C4 Martin
C5 'Land of Hope and Glory'
C6 La Di Da; Gloria
C7 Miss Jones
C8 Medicine
C9 Vienna
C10 Rag and bone men
C11 Hercules
C12 Wilfrid Brambell and Harry H. Corbett
C13 James Hacker; Sir Humphrey Appleby
C14 Olive
C15 Jack

Comedians

D1 *Variety Parade*
D2 Eric Bartholomew and Ernest Wiseman
D3 Glenda Jackson
D4 Angela Rippon
D5 The Management
D6 Lenny Henry and Ade Edmondson
D7 *Murder Most Horrid*; *Absolutely Fabulous*
D8 *Not the Nine O'Clock News*
D9 *Colin's Sandwich*
D10 *Jeeves and Wooster*
D11 'Ooh, you are awful – but I like you!'
D12 The Queen Mother
D13 *Sorry!*
D14 23 Railway Cuttings, East Cheam
D15 Sid James

General Comedy

E1 John Sullivan
E2 127 Nelson Mandela House, Peckham
E3 The Nag's Head where the landlord is Mike
E4 Yellow, with the words Trotters Independent Trading Co., New York, Paris, Peckham
E5 Cassandra
E6 'Lovely jubbly'
E7 Onslow
E8 He was a senior manager within the Finance and General Services Department of the local authority
E9 Emmet and Elizabeth
E10 'The Bouquet residence. The lady of the house speaking.'
E11 Daisy, Rose and Violet
E12 Sheridan, after the eighteenth-century English playwright Richard Brinsley Butler Sheridan
E13 Mrs Councillor Nugent
E14 Her candlelight suppers
E15 Needlework

F1 Nellie
F2 Oswald; a vicar
F3 Lilo Lill and they used to meet in the shed on the allotments
F4 The Whitbury Leisure Centre
F5 Carole
F6 In the High Street on a hospital bed which was part of a students' rag week procession
F7 Malcolm Stoneway and Brenda Wilson
F8 She played Nursie to Elizabeth I (Miranda Richardson)
F9 Lucinda Davis
F10 Pamela
F11 René and Edith Artois
F12 His officer Helga Geerhart
F13 *The Fallen Madonna with the Big Boobies*
F14 Crabtree and 'Good Moaning'
F15 The Resistance is led by Michelle who is often heard to say: 'Listen carefully, I will say this only once.'

G1 *The Golden Girls*
G2 Rowan Atkinson who starred as Blackadder and Mr Bean
G3 Bob
G4 Baldrick
G5 Rik Mayall
G6 General Hogmanay Melchett
G7 Captain Darling
G8 The team were compelled to mount an assault on the enemy and climbed out of the trenches to face certain death
G9 Maplins
G10 Peggy
G11 Squadron leader Clive Dempster
G12 Barry and Yvonne
G13 Garth
G14 Armed robbery
G15 George Hamilton

H1 'I don't believe it.'
H2 He was a security officer
H3 Margaret
H4 Angus Deayton
H5 Mrs Warboys
H6 He wore a blindfold to cut out the light from a street lamp that had crashed through the bedroom window
H7 He came to the rescue of the elderly who were being mistreated in an old people's home
H8 Margaret tried to hide Victor by putting a large flower-pot over his head
H9 Bayview; Harvey Bains
H10 Tom Ballard and Diana Trent
H11 Basil
H12 Matron Jane was shattered when Harvey came home from the ball and announced his engagement to Lucy Maitland
H13 A Mini
H14 He got a turkey jammed on his head
H15 He put his swimming trunks over the top of his trousers and then removed his trousers by sliding them off from underneath

I1   Fashion PR
I2   Fashion editor on a glossy magazine
I3   Lacroix
I4   They mistook their holiday destination and stayed in a basic
     cottage instead of a posh house up the road
I5   Talcum powder
I6   Bubble
I7   A flotation tank
I8   Hywel Bennett
I9   Shelley's wife was Fran and their daughter was Emma
I10 A PhD in geography
I11 Dennis Waterman
I12 Mrs Wembley, who is often heard to say 'just the one' to a
     glass of sherry
I13 A car hire business
I14 *Home James!*
I15 A barber's shop

J1   Hannah and Joe
J2   Richard
J3   Defor (as in D for dog)
J4   A plumber
J5   Margaret Thatcher
J6   They thought they were going to be caught in a hurricane
     and spent a night sheltering in a hotel bathroom
J7   Just before the wedding David was rushed to hospital
     suffering from tetanus
J8   He was a footballer whose career was cut short through
     injury
J9   On a tunnel of love fairground ride
J10 Holmfirth
J11 Nora Batty; wrinkled stockings
J12 He wanted to have his photograph taken in Nora Batty's
     bedroom
J13 Bridlington
J14 Jean Alexander
J15 Manager of a Co-op furniture department

US Comedy

K1 Becky
K2 Connor
K3 Lanford
K4 Boston
K5 Cliff
K6 Danny DeVito
K7 Rose
K8 Dorothy (Bea Arthur)
K9 The Cunninghams
K10 Theo
K11 *The Mary Tyler Moore Show*
K12 Window dresser; New York
K13 Carlton
K14 McGillicuddy
K15 He was a Cuban band leader

Comedy Crossword

Comedy Wordsearch

1 Barbara
2 John Inman
3 Carla Lane
4 Becky
5 Honor Blackman
6 Sybil
7 Slade
8 Chigwell
9 Birdwatching
10 Farnaby
11 Paul Merton
12 Nora Batty
13 *The Wonder Years*
14 Alan B'Stard
15 Raw Sex

Comedy Star Anagrams

1 Richard Briers
2 Patricia Routledge
3 Paul Eddington
4 Ronnie Barker
5 Arthur Lowe
6 John Cleese
7 Mel Smith
8 Jean Boht
9 Hywel Bennett
10 Eric Sykes
11 Nicholas Lyndhurst
12 Michael Crawford
13 James Bolam
14 Warren Mitchell
15 Gareth Hale

COLOURFUL CHARACTERS

1 *To the Manor Born*
2 *Yes, Minister*
3 *All Creatures Great and Small*
4 *Fortunes of War*
5 *L.A. Law*
6 *Casualty*
7 *The Bill*
8 *The Brittas Empire*
9 *Soldier, Soldier*
10 *The Upper Hand*
11 *Cheers*
12 *Waiting for God*
13 *Bread*
14 *Big Deal*
15 *Tinker Tailor Soldier Spy*

THE DETECTIVES

A1 Seaport and Newtown and the real town was Liverpool

A2 Colin Welland played PC Graham and wrote the script to *Chariots of Fire*

A3 Geoffrey Hayes, who played PC Scatliff went on to become the front man with Bungle, Zippy and George

A4 Charlie Barlow and John Watt

A5 He was nicknamed Fancy because he fancied himself as a bit of a hard man

A6 It was named after Sweeney Todd, the rhyming slang for Flying Squad

A7 Chief Inspector Frank Haskins

A8 Stephanie Turner starred in *Juliet Bravo*. Waterman's role was George Carter

A9 Morecambe and Wise

A10 'You're nicked.'

A11 Criminal Intelligence 5 (CI5)

A12 Bodie had served with the SAS and the Parachute Regiment while Doyle was a former CID officer

A13 George Cowley; Gordon Jackson

A14 The Bisto Kids

A15 Shaw took on the role of Chief Constable Alan Cade in *The Chief*

B1 Radio West

B2 Liz Crowther; Leslie Crowther

B3 He was a former mental patient

B4 *A Sense of Guilt*; Felix Cramer

B5 Hartley, Lancashire. Inspector Jean Darblay and Inspector Kate Longdon

B6 Seven Dials police station was located near London's Soho district

B7 Jill Gascoine; *C.A.T.S Eyes*

B8 *The Blue Lamp* (1950)

B9 Mary; Detective Andy Crawford

B10 'Evenin' all'

B11 New York

B12 Cambridge; science

B13 Michael Brandon and Glynis Barber

B14 Ian Hogg
B15 *Rockcliffe's Folly*

C1   Real ale
C2   She was the pathologist
C3   Chief Superintendent Strange
C4   He never married because he never recovered from the
     heartbreak of being jilted in his student days
C5   He hates the sight of blood
C6   Nicole Burgess was an opera singer
C7   Aidensfield; Yorkshire
C8   Claude Jeremiah Greengrass
C9   Sergeant Blaketon is played by Derek Fowlds who was Basil
     Brush's partner and who also appeared as Bernard Wooley in
     Yes, Minister
C10 Miss Lemon
C11 His moustache
C12 203 Whitehaven Mansions
C13 Michael Gambon; *The Singing Detective*
C14 Georges Simenon was born in Belgium
C15 Rupert Davies

D1   Adam Dalgleish
D2   P.D. James
D3   Jimmy Nail; *Auf Wiedersehen, Pet*
D4   Stick
D5   She was blown up while getting into Spender's car
D6   Kingsmarkham
D7   Detective Inspector Mike Burden
D8   Glasgow
D9   Jean and Alison
D10 Mike Jardine
D11 He carved them up and recycled them in black puddings and
     haggis
D12 The Bureau Des Etrangers
D13 Charlie Hungerford; Terence Alexander
D14 Philippa Vale
D15 He went to live with Danielle Aubrey in Provence, France,
     and became a private investigator

E1 Sun Hill
E2 A set was built behind bars because the script called for
    Dashwood to come face to face with a panther
E3 Reg Hollis
E4 Charles Brownlow
E5 Tuesday, 16 October 1984
E6 It became a three-times-a-week series
E7 Sierra Oscar
E8 She was shot dead by a robber's bullet
E9 He became involved in one brawl too many
E10 He was blown up by a car bomb
E11 The bones had been imported from the Philippines for use
     by medical students
E12 Barry Foster; Amsterdam
E13 'Eye Level' by the Simon Park Orchestra was Number One
     for four weeks
E14 Professor Moriarty
E15 The Reichenbach Falls

F1 The Complaints Investigation Bureau
F2 Harry Naylor and Maureen Connell
F3 Angela Berridge; Francesca Annis
F4 The second series did not focus so heavily on Clark's love life
F5 Robbie Coltrane played Fitz in *Cracker*
F6 Psychologist
F7 Bilborough
F8 Panhandle
F9 Smoking, drinking and gambling
F10 *Edge of Darkness*
F11 Roger Moore and Ian Ogilvy
F12 *The Chinese Detective*
F13 *The X Y Y Man*
F14 *No Hiding Place*
F15 They all had Number One hit singles

G1 Christine and Mary Beth
G2 Joyce Davenport
G3 Los Angeles
G4 Huggy Bear
G5 Bing Crosby
G6 Peter Falk
G7 Lollipops
G8 Manhattan's South Precinct
G9 Telly Savalas and George Savalas, who played the roles, were brothers
G10 Sonny Crockett and Ricardo Tubbs
G11 Footballer
G12 Alligator
G13 Sergeant Suzanne 'Pepper' Anderson; Angie Dickinson
G14 Farrah Fawcett-Majors
G15 Joseph (Rocky) Rockford; Sergeant Dennis Becker

The Crime-busters Crossword

The Detectives Wordsearch

The missing detective is T.J. Hooker

COMMERCIAL BREAK

A1   Gibbs SR Toothpaste

A2   Sooty

A3   Bernard Matthews

A4   Campari

A5   Joanna Lumley

A6   Nicole

A7   Coca-Cola

A8   Double Diamond

A9   National Benzole

A10   A minty bit

A11   A woolly jumper

A12   They'd pick up a can of beans and say 'Beanz meanz Heinz'

A13 The Milk Marketing Board
A14 Cinzano
A15 Sebastian Coe; Horlicks

CATCHPHRASES

1 Private Frazer in *Dad's Army*
2 Inspector Blake in *On the Buses*
3 Dixon in *Dixon of Dock Green*
4 Kojak
5 Steve McGarrett in *Hawaii Five-O*
6 Jimmy Savile
7 Annie in *Sitting Pretty*
8 Victor Meldrew in *One Foot in the Grave*
9 The Two Ronnies
10 Valerie Singleton on *Blue Peter*
11 Eric Morecambe
12 Dave Allen
13 Paul Daniels
14 Vic Reeves
15 Ken Dodd

DRAMA

A1 Blackwall
A2 Sicknote got his nickname because he is a hypochondriac; Vaseline was so-called because he was a slippery character
A3 Blue Watch
A4 Marion
A5 He died during an attempt to rescue the driver of a truck that had plunged into the water at Surrey Docks
A6 Sicknote took over the catering and upset the men with his health-food menu
A7 Jack Rosenthal; Maureen Lipman
A8 Ballroom dancing
A9 They were buried under rubble when the wall of a building collapsed on to the truck they were underneath while searching for a hydrant

A10 Technique

A11 She told him that she probably wasn't pregnant after all

A12 Colin came to put out a fire at Zoe's lodgings

A13 They formed an arch by holding up their firemen's axes

A14 He was dubbed Poison Pearce because he is ambitious and does not mind stepping on a few toes

A15 A hearse

B1 Holby City

B2 Julian Chapman and Sandra Nicholl

B3 Charge Nurse

B4 Brenda Fricker; *My Left Foot*

B5 Ewart Plimmer

B6 Edwina Currie claimed that it was propaganda because no casualty department was really that busy

B7 There was a riot and the hospital was set on fire

B8 She was desperate to become pregnant

B9 Robson Green who played porter Jimmy Powell joined the cast of *Soldier, Soldier*

B10 The King's Fusiliers

B11 The King's Fusiliers was merged with another regiment to form the King's Own Fusiliers

B12 The King's Fusiliers wanted to retain the feather badge on their hats – and after a battle were successful in doing so

B13 Nancy went on an officer's training course in England, leaving Paddy behind on his overseas posting

B14 Macaulay

B15 A tattoo on his bottom

C1 1979

C2 The Winchester

C3 A VAT (vodka and tonic)

C4 Plod

C5 Detective Sergeant Chisholm

C6 Terry McCann was a former boxer

C7 'A nice little earner'

C8 Ray Daley was Arthur's nephew

C9 To claim a multi-million pound inheritance from his long-lost Uncle Joshua

C10 Lady Jane Felsham

C11 In a four-poster bed in Scotland
C12 Victoria Cavero; Joanna Lumley
C13 Charlotte Cavendish; auctioneer
C14 Tinker and Eric – who was replaced by Beth Taylor
C15 Jeans, T-shirt and cowboy boots

D1 1920s
D2 Beatrice and Evangeline Eliott
D3 Their father died leaving huge debts, forcing the girls to earn a living by setting up a fashion business
D4 Paris
D5 He became a film director
D6 Montford was a Treasury Minister who was already married
D7 *Upstairs, Downstairs*; the maid, Rose
D8 Fireman
D9 Texas Rangers
D10 Harry Crawford
D11 Rocky Cassidy
D12 Salter was a journalist running a provincial news agency
D13 Arkenfield
D14 Cliff Richard sang the theme tune called 'More to Life'
D15 The money was spent on ten thoroughbred racehorses. Some of the horses were actually in real races and prize money helped pay for their keep

E1 *Peak Practice*
E2 Doctor Jack Kerruish
E3 Timothy Spall
E4 Barry; Frank Stubbs
E5 Adam Faith
E6 Zoë Wanamaker; Tessa Piggott
E7 Kent
E8 Oscar
E9 Tax Inspector
E10 Perfick
E11 Tom and Pat Hollingsworth
E12 Sean Maguire; *EastEnders*; Aidan
E13 Jan Francis
E14 *Lady Chatterley*
E15 *Strathblair*

Vintage Drama

F1   Robert Powell; Jasper Carrott
F2   Charles Ryder; painter
F3   Castle Howard, Yorkshire
F4   Lord Marchmain; Laurence Olivier
F5   Aloysius
F6   Hari Kumar; Art Malik
F7   Ronald Merrick
F8   Mrs Bridges
F9   Gordon Jackson (Hudson) went on to play George Cowley in *The Professionals*
F10 The Bellamys
F11 John Alderton and Pauline Collins; *Forever Green*
F12 *Edward the Seventh*; the Queen
F13 Timothy West; Prunella Scales
F14 Keith Michell
F15 Annette Crosbie; Dorothy Tutin; Anne Stallybrass; Elvi Hale; Angela Pleasence; Rosalie Crutchley

G1   American
G2   *Another Bouquet*
G3   Captain Baines
G4   The *Charlotte Rhodes*
G5   *The Forsyte Saga*
G6   She caused a stir in her leather suits and 'kinky' boots
G7   They both became Bond girls
G8   Bill Simpson
G9   Tannochbrae
G10 Arden House
G11 Simon Templar; Roger Moore and Ian Ogilvy
G12 The Mermaid Yard
G13 Ken Masters
G14 *Tutti Frutti*
G15 Tricki Woo

US Drama

H1　Rudy and Tom Jordache; Peter Strauss and Nick Nolte
H2　The Ingalls
H3　*Bonanza*
H4　*The Winds of War*
H5　Kunta Kinte
H6　Chicken George; cock-fighting
H7　Father Ralph de Bricassart; Richard Chamberlain
H8　The American Civil War
H9　John Boy; journalism
H10　David Janssen; Dr Richard Kimble
H11　*Lace*
H12　1965
H13　Mia Farrow and Ryan O'Neal
H14　Constance Mackenzie
H15　The New York Academy of Performing Arts

Guess the Drama Shows

1　*London's Burning*
2　*The House of Eliott*
3　*The Onedin Line*
4　*The Waltons*
5　*The Saint*
6　*The Avengers*
7　*Making Out*
8　*Pennies from Heaven*
9　*Growing Pains*
10　*A Year in Provence*
11　*All Creatures Great and Small*
12　*Auf Wiedersehen, Pet*
13　*A Time to Dance*
14　*Fortunes of War*
15　*Reilly, Ace of Spies*

Drama Wordsearch

1 Robert Powell
2 Eaton Place
3 Evelyn Waugh
4 India
5 Timothy West
6 Soames
7 Patrick Swayze
8 Alex Haley
9 Publisher
10 John Steed
11 Rula Lenska
12 The Winchester
13 John Boy
14 *Wings*
15 The Cavendish

SUPERCOOKS

A1 Fanny and Johnny Cradock
A2 The Galloping Gourmet
A3 *The Food and Drink Show*
A4 Keith Floyd
A5 Rustie Lee
A6 Susan Brookes
A7 Loyd Grossman
A8 Madhur Jaffrey
A9 Chris Kelly
A10 *Grow Your Greens* and *Eat Your Greens*
A11 Delia Smith
A12 Michael Barry
A13 Mireille Johnston
A14 Ruth Mott
A15 *Chef!*; Lenny Henry; Gareth Blackstock

TOP OF THE POPS

A1 1964
A2 A converted church in Manchester; Jimmy Savile
A3 Pan's People
A4 'Je T'Aime' by Jane Birkin and Serge Gainsbourg
A5 'Relax' by Frankie Goes to Hollywood
A6 David Jacobs
A7 Pete Murray
A8 Susan Stranks; *Magpie*
A9 Noel Edmonds
A10 Freddie Mills
A11 Josephine Douglas
A12 Adam Faith
A13 Cliff Richard
A14 *Boy Meets Girls*
A15 *Ready, Steady, Go!*

B1 Cliff Richard
B2 Bob Geldof
B3 Lulu

B4   Elton John
B5   'It's Not Unusual'
B6   *The Partridge Family*
B7   Davy Jones; *Coronation Street*, as Ena Sharples' grandson
B8   Bill Haley
B9   Madness
B10   Engelbert Humperdinck
B11   'Love of the Loved'; Number thirty-five
B12   *Sex*
B13   Elton John
B14   'Ashes to Ashes'
B15   'Love Me Do'

C1   'Suicide is Painless'
C2   Prince
C3   Wilfrid Brambell and Harry H. Corbett
C4   Rod Stewart; 'Sailing'
C5   Peter Polycarpou; Chris in *Birds of a Feather*
C6   'Whispering Grass'
C7   Anita Dobson
C8   Jason Donovan
C9   Emma Wray who plays Brenda
C10   'With a Little Help from My Friends'
C11   'The Floral Dance'; Number twenty-one
C12   'Stairway to Heaven'
C13   *The Young Ones*
C14   'I Could Be So Good for You'; Dennis Waterman
C15   Bono of U2

Popagram

1 Elton John
2 Mick Jagger
3 Tina Turner
4 Cliff Richard
5 Michael Jackson
6 Annie Lennox
7 Madonna
8 Jason Donovan
9 Mick Hucknall
10 Elvis Presley
11 Tom Jones
12 Stevie Wonder
13 David Bowie
14 Paul McCartney
15 Sinead O'Connor

Chart-Toppers Wordsearch

1 Elvis Presley
2 The Beatles
3 Rod Stewart
4 T. Rex
5 Abba
6 The Police
7 Blondie
8 Band Aid
9 The Rolling Stones
10 The Boomtown Rats
11 Cliff Richard
12 Queen
13 Michael Jackson
14 Whitney Houston
15 Take That

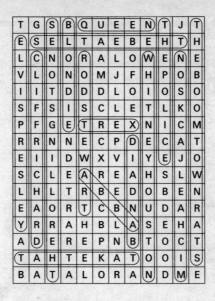

THE BIG SCREEN

A1 Flying bicycles
A2 Plumber
A3 Morticia
A4 *Back to the Future*
A5 The Dead Poets Society
A6 *Dick Tracy*
A7 *Hook*; Peter Pan
A8 Edward Scissorhands
A9 *Home Alone*
A10 Clark Kent; Lois Lane
A11 Bruce Willis
A12 Arnold Schwarzenegger and Danny DeVito
A13 He laughed like a hyena
A14 He made a wish on a fairground machine

A15   *Butch Cassidy and the Sundance Kid.* The song was
       'Raindrops Keep Fallin' on My Head'

B1   The Sheriff of Nottingham threatened to call off Christmas
       in *Robin Hood: Prince of Thieves*
B2   Empire State Building, New York
B3   She set up as a manufacturer of baby food
B4   *Sister Act*
B5   Ice-cream
B6   He played the Joker in *Batman*
B7   Her head
B8   Robin Williams
B9   *Gremlins*
B10   Marshmallow
B11   The Holy Grail
B12   *Honey, I Shrunk the Kids*
B13   *Ghost*; Patrick Swayze
B14   A shoe shop
B15   *Carry on Henry*

C1   An ice-pick
C2   Elm Street (*Nightmare on Elm Street*)
C3   *Apocalypse Now*
C4   *Cape Fear*
C5   The ship's cat
C6   She killed it and left it cooking in a pot on the stove
C7   *The French Connection*
C8   The greenhouse
C9   A million dollars to spend the night with his wife (Demi
       Moore)
C10   *The Terminator*; Arnold Schwarzenegger
C11   Bo Derek
C12   Buffalo Bill
C13   Marlon Brando
C14   Champagne, a cigarette and matches
C15   *The Lover* (Jane March)

D1 *Gentlemen Prefer Blondes*
D2 *A Fistful of Dollars*
D3 *The African Queen*
D4 *Breakfast at Tiffany's*
D5 *Calamity Jane*
D6 Sam Spade
D7 Johnny Weissmuller
D8 *All About Eve*
D9 Maurice Chevalier in *Gigi*
D10 Harvey
D11 Boris Karloff
D12 *The Dam Busters*
D13 Dr Simon Sparrow; Brigitte Bardot
D14 Clark Gable as Rhett Butler in *Gone with the Wind*
D15 Yul Brynner, Steve McQueen, Charles Bronson, James
    Coburn, Brad Dexter, Robert Vaughn and Horst Buchholz

E1 Barrister
E2 A cello
E3 A pig
E4 Carl Bernstein and Bob Woodward
E5 Patrick Swayze and Jennifer Grey
E6 *Robin Hood: Prince of Thieves*; (Everything I Do) 'I Do It for
    You'; Bryan Adams
E7 Jane Fonda in *Barbarella*
E8 *Dr No* in 1962
E9 They ran out of the church and jumped on a bus
E10 *The Last Emperor*
E11 *The Firm*
E12 Barbra Streisand
E13 *Chariots of Fire*
E14 Roxane
E15 *Holiday Inn*

- F1 She had a hole in her middle
- F2 Horticulturist
- F3 *Cabaret*
- F4 His bowler hat
- E5 *Dangerous Liaisons*
- F6 *Ghostbusters*
- F7 Dr Richard Kimble
- F8 He had only one arm
- F9 A severed hand
- F10 The Whistle Stop Café
- F11 *Gandhi*
- F12 Her bikini top
- F13 Robin Williams; *Good Morning, Vietnam*
- F14 As a film camera
- F15 *Citizen Kane*

The Big Screen Crossword

The Big Screen Wordsearch

1 Scaramanga
2 Baloo
3 McFly
4 Hannibal Lecter
5 Sam
6 Callahan
7 Jessica
8 Mrs Robinson
9 Eliot Ness
10 Clyde
11 Darth Vader
12 Virgil Tibbs
13 Lurch
14 Damien
15 Norman Bates
16 Sandy
17 Eliza Doolittle
18 Mr T

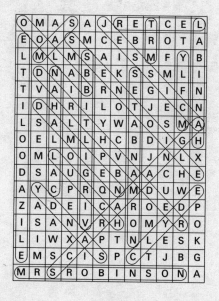

119

NAME GAME

A1 Robbie
A2 Theo
A3 Norman Stanley
A4 Sidney
A5 Simon
A6 Ernest
A7 Frank
A8 Dave and Ken
A9 Jim and Harriet
A10 Robert T
A11 James
A12 Lisa
A13 Alfred (Tosh is his nickname)
A14 Eddie
A15 Alan
A16 Jules
A17 David
A18 Hercule
A19 Piet
A20 Reg

GAME SHOWS

A1 Henry Kelly
A2 *Every Second Counts*; Paul Daniels
A3 Norwich
A4 Anthea Redfern
A5 Larry Grayson; Isla St Clair
A6 Carol Dilworth
A7 1956; Hughie Green
A8 Bob Monkhouse
A9 Jerry Desmonde
A10 *Spot the Tune*
A11 Schoolteacher
A12 *Catchphrase*
A13 A *Blankety Blank* chequebook and pen
A14 *Endurance*
A15 *Trick or Treat* and *Sticky Moments*

Game for a Laugh

 1 Bruce Forsyth
 2 Bob Monkhouse
 3 Bob Holness
 4 Anneka Rice
 5 Chris Tarrant
 6 Noel Edmonds
 7 Gordon Burns
 8 Richard Madeley
 9 Michael Aspel
10 Henry Kelly
11 Cilla Black
12 Jim Bowen
13 Les Dawson
14 Leslie Crowther
15 Nicky Campbell

Game Show Wordsearch

1 Terry Wogan
2 Dusty Bin
3 Larry Grayson
4 Carol Smillie
5 Snooker
6 Michael Miles
7 The Gold Run
8 *Catchphrase*
9 Second
10 Bernie
11 Nine
12 Nicholas Parsons
13 Tune
14 Max Bygraves
15 *Strike It Lucky*

OUT OF THIS WORLD

A1   1963
A2   Susan
A3   Time and Relative Dimension in Space
A4   William Hartnell
A5   Tom Baker
A6   Jon Pertwee
A7   Gallifrey
A8   *The Quatermass Experiment*
A9   Sulu
A10 Chief Engineer Lieutenant Commander Montgomery 'Scotty' Scott
A11 The Incredible Hulk
A12 *Blake's 7*
A13 Behind Del Floria's tailor shop in Manhattan
A14 David McCallum
A15 United Network Command for Law Enforcement

B1   Diane
B2   Bruce Wayne; Adam West
B3   Gotham City
B4   Burgess Meredith
B5   Submarine
B6   International Rescue
B7   The Hood
B8   Lady Penelope
B9   FAB 1
B10 *Doomwatch*
B11 *Survivors*
B12 *The Champions*
B13 Patrick McGoohan
B14 Number Two
B15 Portmeirion, North Wales

Sci-Fi Wordsearch

1 Green
2 Robin Williams
3 USS *Enterprise*
4 *Quantum Leap*
5 Lee Majors
6 Scott Tracy
7 *Doctor Who*
8 Mr Spock
9 Daleks
10 Gerry Anderson
11 Troy Tempest
12 Napoleon Solo
13 Dr Peter Brady
14 Diana Rigg
15 Atlantis

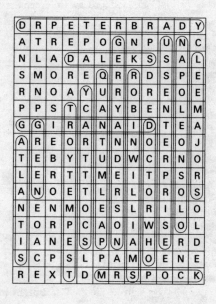

THE SOAPS

Coronation Street

A1 Minnie Caldwell and Martha Longhurst
A2 James Callaghan
A3 Martha Longhurst
A4 Martin Shaw
A5 Her grandson and son-in-law had been killed in a car crash
A6 She was electrocuted by a faulty hairdryer plug
A7 Leonard Swindley; Arthur Lowe
A8 He was murdered by gunmen during an armed robbery at Mike Baldwin's warehouse
A9 Hilda had forgotten to post his coupon
A10 He was run over by a tram in Blackpool
A11 Torremolinos; a waitress
A12 Kevin Webster
A13 He drilled through the ceiling and into Reg Holdsworth's water bed
A14 She had a tipsy fling with Curly Watts
A15 He put tennis raquets on his feet and walked round and round to create 'corn circles' in the long grass in Des's garden

Brookside

B1 The toilet
B2 Dicken Ashworth; *Coronation Street* as Jeff Horton
B3 Matty Nolan
B4 At a guest house in Llandudno
B5 Tommy McArdle
B6 Annabelle Collins
B7 Peter Montague
B8 On the electronic scoreboard at Goodison Park, home of Everton Football Club
B9 His *Gay Times* was delivered to the Corkhills by mistake
B10 He was a heroin addict
B11 He was stabbed to death in York

B12　Brian Lawrence
B13　Barry Grant
B14　Susannah; Matthew and Emily
B15　La Luz

Emmerdale

C1　Jacob Sugden
C2　*Field of Tares*
C3　Sam and Sally
C4　Gun-running
C5　Stealing Christmas trees
C6　A cartload of horse manure was dumped in the Woolpack car park
C7　His daughter Annie
C8　His associate Derek Walker
C9　Graham Lodsworth; Ross Kemp; Grant in *EastEnders*
C10　For leading a protest against a nuclear dump
C11　He was crushed to death by Joe Sugden's prize bull
C12　Lynn Whiteley
C13　Phil Redmond
C14　Josh Lewis
C15　A prostitute

Dallas and Dynasty

D1　Southfork
D2　At a Ewing barbeque; New Orleans
D3　Ewing 3
D4　Sue Ellen; Kristin Shepard
D5　Digger Barnes
D6　In a helicopter crash in South America
D7　Cally Harper
D8　The Hot Biscuit
D9　Ray Krebbs
D10　Mark Graison
D11　Head of Public Relations

D12 Denver

D13 Jeff Colby

D14 Alexis 'accidentally' fired a gun and the horse Krystle was riding bolted and threw her off

D15 Mark Jennings; congressman Neal McVane

Neighbours

E1 Paul Robinson was married to convicted killer Terri Inglis

E2 Charlene and Henry

E3 Paul

E4 Harold Bishop

E5 Christina and Caroline Alessi

E6 Todd was rushing to the clinic to prevent Phoebe from having an abortion

E7 Jill Weir

E8 An engagement ring

E9 Tickets to see a Michael Jackson concert

E10 Hannah's doll

E11 He tried to drown her in the Jacuzzi

E12 Jim suffered a massive heart attack

E13 Beth persuaded Brad to become more than just a good friend

E14 Bouncer

E15 Craig McLachlan

Home and Away

F1 They thought they were unable to have children of their own

F2 Roo Stewart jilted him because he wasn't the father of her child

F3 Carly Morris

F4 Marilyn

F5 Meg died from leukaemia in Blake's arms on the beach

F6 Donald Fisher and Morag Bellingham

F7 Steven

F8 Al Simpson

F9 She was blackmailed by a photographer over sexy pictures from her past

F10 Because he was framed for a robbery

F11 He received fatal injuries when he was involved in an accident with another car driven recklessly by Karen

F12 She suffered head injuries after being hit by a speedboat

F13 Tamara; David

F14 Dale was a cot death victim

F15 Sam threw a stick at Adam's head

EastEnders

G1 Walford

G2 Dirty Den Watts

G3 Angie Watts

G4 Gill married Mark Fowler just before dying from AIDS

G5 Gretna Green

G6 Grant Mitchell

G7 Pat was put in prison for drink-driving after an accident in which a girl was killed

G8 He married Romanian Nadia to prevent her from being deported

G9 Michelle's daughter Vicki was abducted

G10 A knee injury

G11 He died in a car crash

G12 Christine Hewitt

G13 The death of Ian's father, Pete Beale

G14 He laced her food with poison

G15 Eddie Royle

The Soaps Crossword

Across / Down grid filled as:

```
B R A D ■ M I K E R E I D
L ■ ■ ■ T ■ S ■ V ■ W ■ ■
A I L S A ■ A M E R I C A
K ■ O ■ X ■ B ■ N ■ N ■ I
E L U S I V E ■ I ■ G A S
■ ■ ■ ■ L ■ N ■ N ■ ■ ■ L
S T E A M Y ■ I G N O R E
P ■ ■ A ■ A ■ ■ ■ ■ ■ ■ ■
E N A U ■ L E T I T I A ■
E ■ N ■ R ■ E ■ R ■ U ■ G
D A N I E L S ■ A N G I E
■ ■ I ■ E ■ S ■ M ■ ■ ■ N
Q U E E N V I C ■ V E S T
```

The Soaps Wordsearch

Watts	Armstrong
Sullivan	Stewart
Holdsworth	Ross
Fowler	Marshall
Mitchell	Carpenter
Tavernier	Burke
Rogers	Mangel
Dixon	Ewing
Corkhill	Farlow
Sugden	Krebbs
Brooks	

M	H	O	L	D	S	W	O	R	T	H	F
A	E	R	D	G	N	I	W	E	L	G	C
R	O	M	I	T	C	H	E	L	L	F	O
M	L	P	E	A	R	N	T	W	A	A	R
S	J	O	F	V	O	R	C	O	H	R	K
T	R	O	G	E	R	S	D	F	S	L	H
R	L	R	D	R	A	B	C	H	R	O	I
O	S	E	I	N	S	B	A	F	A	W	L
N	R	S	X	I	U	E	R	K	M	R	L
G	P	D	O	E	L	R	P	X	E	T	O
N	O	R	N	R	L	K	E	K	R	U	B
A	S	E	T	E	I	O	N	E	S	A	R
M	T	C	G	A	V	S	T	A	R	S	O
C	T	N	T	R	A	W	E	T	S	I	O
O	A	R	O	L	N	A	R	E	N	R	K
M	W	O	R	S	U	G	D	E	N	E	S

Soapagrams

1 Percy Sugden
2 Bet Gilroy
3 Mavis Wilton
4 Arthur Fowler
5 Pat Butcher
6 Kathy Beale
7 Madge Bishop
8 Doug Willis
9 Mick Johnson
10 Patricia Farnham
11 Joe Sugden
12 Frank Tate
13 JR Ewing
14 Cliff Barnes
15 Krystle Carrington

ADVENTURE

A1   Korea
A2   Haiti's Papa Doc Duvalier
A3   Armand and Michaela Denis
A4   *Zoo Quest*
A5   Jacques Cousteau
A6   *Calypso*
A7   *Life on Earth*
A8   Spitsbergen; seventeen countries
A9   Fourteen
A10 *Don't Ask Me*
A11 *Survival*
A12 Bristol
A13 Hans and Lotte Hass
A14 *Life in the Freezer*
A15 007 actor Timothy Dalton

TELEVISION BUFF'S CHALLENGE

A1   Poirot (David Suchet)
A2   *The Likely Lads* and *Whatever Happened to the Likely Lads?*
A3   Her collar-bone
A4   She might never wear strapless dresses again
A5   Noeline
A6   *Bonanza*
A7   *Rawhide*
A8   Patrick Duffy starred in *Dallas* and *The Man from Atlantis* in which he had webbed fingers and toes
A9   Sam Butcher
A10 Bob Landers
A11 The Mayfair Academy of Modelling in Croydon
A12 *Danger Man*
A13 Kylie
A14 Onslow, who never wears a shirt, so his vest reveals a large tattoo on each arm
A15 The Barker-Finches

B1   Trotters Independent Trading Co
B2   Boycie is married to Marlene and Trigger is his sidekick
B3   Racquel became Del's live-in lady and they named their son
     Damian
B4   The Baumblatt Foundation
B5   St Isaac's cathedral in St Petersburg in Russia
B6   *Love Hurts* star Adam Faith played the title role in the
     Seventies series *Budgie*
B7   Wally Batty was passionate about his pigeons
B8   His ferrets
B9   A man arriving in a taxi was rude, so Victor threw his wig
     down the drain
B10 The baby's father resembled the gnome
B11 He was so badly sun-burned he couldn't walk
B12 Geoffrey and Marion
B13 When she was present at the birth of her niece Sarah's baby
B14 *Tenko*
B15 Madge Alsop

C1   Anthony Hopkins played Hannibal Lecter in *The Silence of
     the Lambs* and then made a television special about lions
C2   Derek got left behind at a motorway service station
C3   Under the patio in the garden
C4   She planned to have the baby on Todd's grave
C5   Los Barcos
C6   *The Men's Room*
C7   *Lady Chatterley*
C8   Bertie Wooster
C9   John Major; *Spitting Image*
C10 Gladys Emmanuel
C11 An alarm clock; his trousers
C12 Jane Seymour starred in the Bond film *Live and Let Die* and
     the television series *Dr Quinn: Medicine Woman*
C13 He received a head injury after being flattened by a rubble-
     filled wheelbarrow dropped from scaffolding
C14 Martin and Ann
C15 Howard and Hilda

D1   Vic Reeves

D2   Mr Blobby

D3   *Gladiators*

D4   *'Allo 'Allo*

D5   It was reported that Soo was expecting a baby and there was speculation about Sooty being the father

D6   Tony Clark in *Between the Lines*

D7   Sixteen years

D8   Colin Welland wrote the screenplay for *Chariots of Fire* and played PC David Graham in *Z Cars*

D9   He was shot by a terrorist

D10 They are both set in the Bristol area

D11 Johnny Briggs (Mike Baldwin in *Coronation Street*)

D12 His wife is Louise and he adores her cooking

D13 Opium

D14 Sheena Easton

D15 Angela Lansbury starred in the film *Bedknobs and Broomsticks* and plays Jessica Fletcher in *Murder, She Wrote*

E1   Bobby Charlton – his daughter Suzanne is a television weather forecaster

E2   Gary Lineker spoke Japanese in the football drama *All in the Game*

E3   The Manageress was Gabriella Benson (played by Cherie Lunghi)

E4   Warren Clarke

E5   Elaine (Janet Dibley) and Ashley (Nicholas Lyndhurst)

E6   *After Henry*

E7   'We're going up your stairs.'

E8   Central Television

E9   They both played actresses in an episode of *Tales of the Unexpected* called 'A Girl Can't Always Have Everything'

E10 A frying pan

E11 He made a series of anonymous telephone calls

E12 Two

E13 Craig McLachlan, who appeared in both *Neighbours* and *Home and Away*

E14 Jason Donovan, who won acclaim in the title role of the stage production of *Joseph and the Technicolor Dreamcoat*

E15 'Grandad' was made by *Dad's Army* actor Clive Dunn

F1   Adolf Hitler
F2   Anthony Hopkins
F3   Michael Palin, who sampled a mud bath during his *Pole to Pole* journey
F4   *The Lives and Loves of a She-Devil*
F5   Bob Hoskins; *Pennies from Heaven*
F6   *To Play the King*
F7   Marcus
F8   *Middlemarch*
F9   *The Jewel in the Crown*
F10 Captain Pugwash
F11 Thirteen and three-quarters
F12 Frankie Howerd
F13 Frank Spencer who was played by Michael Crawford
F14 Rigsby in *Rising Damp*
F15 *Monty Python's Flying Circus*

TELEVISION NOSTALGIA PICTURE QUIZ

1 *Do Not Adjust Your Set*; *Open All Hours*; *A Touch of Frost*; *Only Fools and Horses*; *The Darling Buds of May*
2 *No Hiding Place*
3 Designer; free gifts for cereal packets was the last straw
4 Dennis Waterman
5 *Slinger's Day*
6 Patricia Routledge; Hyacinth Bucket in *Keeping Up Appearances*
7 Ian McShane; Lovejoy
8 Purdey; after the gun
9 Cilla Black; 'Anyone Who Had a Heart'
10 Des O'Connor; *Take Your Pick*
11 The slave Lurcio
12 Tony Curtis; *The Persuaders*
13 Noel Edmonds – Lionel was the victim of a Gotcha in *Noel's House Party*
14 She somehow managed to turn in the air, cushion her fall by landing on Dexter and get up and walk away unscathed
15 The woman in the Oxo advert; Helen Herriot in *All Creatures Great and Small*; Faith in *Second Thoughts*
16 A plumber; he discovered a cellar of vintage wine and sold it for a fortune
17 George Cole

SIGNET

Published or forthcoming

DEFINITIVE I.Q. TEST FOR CATS
and
I.Q. TEST FOR CAT OWNERS

Melissa Miller

A brand new edition of the accurate, entertaining assessment of your cat's brainpower.

When your cat is wearing an expression of mystic beauty, is it contemplating the meaning of life, or just wondering what's for dinner? When it winds itself round your legs does it simply want another saucer of milk? And how suitable an owner are you? Do you toss and turn, disturbing puss's valuable beauty sleep? Are you suitably grateful when your cat drops small, dead rodents at your feet? Is your cat an Einstein of the feline world?

FIND OUT IN THIS IRRESISTIBLE, ORIGINAL CAT I.Q. TEST

Four tests for your cat and four for you so that you can check your mutual compatibility or choose a suitable breed of cat for your way of life. Packed with historical and mythological references, literary quotations and a whole new section of reader's humorous anecdotes, this book is a must for all cat owners, potential cat owners and felines everywhere.

CAUTION! USED CARS

Philip D. Turner

Caution! Used Cars is packed with expert, up-to-the-minute information to help you buy a better used car and sell the one you own. You can find out how to:

Ensure a car is roadworthy before you buy it

Learn your rights as a consumer

Guard against buying a stolen or clocked car

and much, much more.

'Straightforward, honest and useful ... Full of sensible advice on when, how and what to purchase' – *Daily Telegraph*

SIGNET

Published or forthcoming

LIFE, LOVE
AND DESTINY

Barbara Dunn and **Archie Dunlop**

Follow this practical, easy-to-use guide to find
out the secrets of the stars and you'll soon be
able to draw up your very own horoscope and
open up a personal hot line to the cosmos.

Discover all you need to look for in a lover – the
stars can tell you what you don't already know!

New insights into everyday life at work and at
home are revealed – say goodbye to confusion
and misunderstanding. With *Life, Love and
Destiny* as your closest companion, you can discover what the future will bring.

SIGNET

Published or forthcoming

YOUR
FAVOURITE SOAPS
PUZZLE & QUIZ BOOK

Chris Pointer and **Alison Fitzpatrick**

Are you switched on to TV soaps? Then here's your chance to find out just how good you really are at remembering the people, plots and personalities from television's most popular shows.

Why did *Coronation Street*'s Derek walk around his neighbour's garden with tennis rackets on his feet?

What unusual illness caused Kathy Bates to miscarry her baby in *Emmerdale*?

How did the assassin disguise the gun that killed Dirty Den in *EastEnders*?

How was *Home and Away*'s Bobby fatally injured?

What happened at Brad and Beth's wedding in *Neighbours*?

As well as quizzes, you'll find crosswords and puzzles and a fantastic photo nostalgia quiz – guaranteed to keep the family entertained for hours!